School Principal's Handbook
of
Evaluation Guidelines

Also by the author:

COMPLETE GUIDE TO CO-CURRICULAR PROGRAMS AND
ACTIVITIES FOR THE MIDDLE GRADES

School Principal's Handbook
of
Evaluation Guidelines

John Frank, Jr.

PARKER PUBLISHING COMPANY, INC.
WEST NYACK, NEW YORK

© 1979 by

PARKER PUBLISHING COMPANY, INC.

West Nyack, N.Y.

Library of Congress Cataloging in Publication Data

Frank, John
   School principal's handbook of evaluation
guidelines.

   Bibliography: p.
   Includes index.
   1. Educational surveys. 2. Middle schools.
3. School superintendents and principals.
I. Title.
LB2846.F69   379'.15   78-20824
ISBN 0-13-794024-6

Printed in the United States of America

DEDICATION

To the memory of my mother

ABOUT THE AUTHOR

John Frank, Jr., at present Assistant Superintendent of Schools for the Hartford School District in White River Junction, Vermont, has had a broad and varied career in education. He has served as a teacher, athletic coach, elementary, junior high, and middle school principal in Connecticut and in Vermont.

He is past recipient of the Danforth/National Academy for School Executives Fellowship for extensive educational study in the United States and in 1979 was awarded the academy's *Professional Development Award*. John Frank, Jr. is also the author of *Complete Guide to Co-Curricular Programs and Activities for the Middle Grades*.

EVALUATION BLUEPRINT FOR ADMINISTRATORS

This book provides a complete, practical program to measure and evaluate every facet of your total school program. It will enable you to become more directly and productively aware of those factors, hidden as well as obvious, that contribute to total school success.

You will discover the best practices of 25 carefully selected school districts and dozens of individuals, who are actively involved with various phases of school evaluation. Here are just a few of the things you'll be able to accomplish as a result of reading and *using* this book:

- Identify appropriate evaluation techniques for your school.
- Develop a school evaluation model that will fit your particular needs.
- Be reasonably sure that provisions have been made to effectively evaluate *all* components of the total school operation.
- Involve the total school staff in the evaluation process.
- Promote evaluation as an integral part of the school curriculum and instruction program.

These evaluation guidelines offer you a real opportunity to expand instructional horizons. When appropriately applied as a tool to improve the quality of instruction, they will enable you . . .

1. To insure that the student evaluation process provides teachers with a viable means of measuring and improving the actual learning experience.

2. To continue a *consistent* upgrading of the operational effectiveness of your school programs.

You will also be able to use the "Evaluation Time Calendar" to insure that evaluation becomes integrated and coordinated with the teaching-learning process.

In using this book, you will discover that these school evaluation programs offer a common sense approach to futuristic program planning. You will learn how to develop evaluation guidelines to handle increased demands for accountability in the areas of:

- Student basic competency skill attainment.
- Curriculum development and program validation.
- Resource allocation in terms of money, staff, facilities, time and environmental conditions.
- In-service program development and/or revision.
- School goals and objectives.
- Professional staff needs and programs designed to provide for staff development and self-renewal.

Further, *all* essential elements of a sound evaluation program will be identified and discussed to enable you to develop a *complete* program. They will help you save hours of labor trying to envision, create, and develop evaluation activities of your own.

School evaluation guidelines do not have to denote a highly complex computerized, sophisticated operation. Rather, this book offers principals and other administrators the opportuniy to simplify the total school evaluation process and make the most effective use of available resources.

Successful evaluation programs are predicated on close collaboration among school partners—parents, teachers, administrators, other district staff and students. Only through cooperative evaluation of programs can effective action and further guidelines for productive change be established. This book offers practical suggestions for developing the cooperative evaluation spirit necessary for a successful school evaluation program.

External demands continue to erode a principal's ability to function as the *instructional leader* of his school. School evaluation guidelines help to insure a return to that role by showing you how to produce program evaluation results that parents, teachers, students and community can identify with.

You will have an opportunity to explore some of the best evaluation practices known in developing Needs Assessments, Evaluation Teams, Evaluation Models, Measurable Goals and Objectives, Staff Evaluation and Student Evaluation Programs among others. You will find a valuable collection of evaluation guides, charts and forms that can be readily adapted to your local school. The detailed programs are presented so concisely that all you have to do is take them from the book, enabling you to quickly use them as you develop your own evaluation guidelines.

Supportive school services are frequently taken for granted or ignored in most school evaluation programs. This book presents a number of evaluation instruments for custodial, maintenance, food service, transportation, health, social service and other auxiliary services.

Through involvement, identification, planning, allocation of resources and on-going evaluation, you can develop programs that will help you meet the present and future need for increased accountability. This book will show you how.

John Frank, Jr.

ACKNOWLEDGEMENTS

To a number of fine people in the profession who shared their thoughts with me and made materials available. My gratitude to Priscilla Labelle for interpreting my handwriting and typing the manuscript and Mac Hooper for his initial editing.

The following school districts and administrators provided materials for this book and I am grateful to them.

School District Number One, Batesville,
Arkansas   Chapter 2

Eastern Junior High School, Riverside,
Connecticut
Benjamin Davenport, Principal   Chapters 3 & 4

Sarasota County Schools, Florida
Gene Pillot, Superintendent   Chapter 3

Hartford School District, Hartford, Vermont
Frank Kenison and J. Wendell Warren,
Principals   Chapters 3, 4, 5
Floyd McPhetres, Math Department Chairman   Chapters 6, 8, 12

Public Schools, Westport, Connecticut
Kenneth Brummel, Superintendent   Chapter 4

Hampton High School, Hampton, Nebraska
Kenneth W. Hoppner, Superintendent   Chapter 4

Birmingham School District,
Birmingham, Michigan
Donald Peckenpaugh, Superintendent   Chapter 6

Public Schools, Attleboro, Massachusetts
Robert Coehlo, Superintendent   Chapter 7

Alhambra High School, Phoenix, Arizona
Wellesley C. Goodwin, Principal   Chapter 9

Table of Figures

Table of Contents

Needs assessment and goal relationships . . . The principal's
role in goal selection and evaluation . . . Establishing goals
and objectives with staff . . . The principal defines his objectives . . . Creating measurable process objectives . . . Developing the evaluation time frame . . . Reporting goal evaluation
results . . . Revising school goals and objectives based on
evaluation data.

How to evaluate the school planning process . . . The program planning group . . . Evaluating existing programs . . .
The role of evaluation in program development . . . Examin-
ing program evaluation constraints . . . Making provisions for
sequential step evaluations . . . How to evaluate long term
programs.

Ensuring parity with staff representation . . . A sample evaluation team description . . . The principal's role on the evaluation team . . . Setting up the team resource library . . . Preparing for the first meeting . . . Allocating resources to the evaluation team . . . Defining team member roles . . . Setting goal
parameters for the team . . . Establishing communications
guidelines for the team . . . Evaluating team progress.

Determining priorities for evaluation . . . Fitting the model to
the school environment . . . Designing the school evaluation
model . . . How to simplify the evaluation process . . . Examples of evaluation models . . . Evaluating the whole co-
curricular activity program . . . The evaluation matrix . . .
Gaining approval of the school evaluation model.

School Principal's Handbook
of
Evaluation Guidelines

School Evaluation: **1**

Examining Some Prerequisites

IDENTIFYING THE NEED FOR SCHOOL EVALUATION

As schools phase out the decade of 1970's and enter into the era of the 1980's, the demand to evaluate what each school intends to accomplish and the extent to which it is meeting the needs of students and expectations of the community it serves will accentuate. Accountability will become the watchword for schools as demands for greater student productivity increase.

Principals and staff will need to become well-versed and

1

proficient in the use of evaluation skills. Local policies and state mandates will continue to place the burden of proof on schools to show that inputs such as staff, money, curriculum, etc., equal appropriate student outputs—ability to spell, read, write, add, subtract and gain other skills necessary to function in society.

Administrators and teachers will continue to be called up to verify the effectiveness of teachers, programs and school operations. A good portion of the evaluation resources designed for school use today are filled with evaluation jargon. These highly technical terms make it virtually impossible for the average principal or staff to comprehend the process of evaluation; carrying it out becomes even less practical.

Some examples of sophisticated terms include: structural supports, stability coefficients, rank order coefficient, geocode analysis, trend surface analysis, errorless discrimination and responsive evaluation. The list is endless and so are the number of school professionals who have little, if any, idea what these mean or how to use them within their own school setting.

The need arises to identify the school evaluation program as an integral and continuous part of the teaching-learning situation. Evaluation has to be developed as a tool to improve learning—a concept designed to improve the quality of education.

MAJOR PROBLEMS ASSOCIATED WITH SCHOOL EVALUATION

Most school evaluation focuses on the informal approach, i.e., observations, visits, conferences, teacher opinions and others. Formal evaluation is often avoided and seldom used unless it is essential to meet pressures for accountability. Experiences with formal evaluations in the past have often been discouraging and rated as non-productive by many schools because the results have a tendency to show that no significant difference occurs when new programs are implemented. Often the internal and external factors that need to be changed by the program are so ingrained and pronounced that the amount of change possible is negligible. This does not preclude, however, that new programs are not necessary or valuable.

The number of educators who have sufficient training in evaluation is limited; consequently, the quality of evaluation from within is usually less than adequate. Administrators are often suspicious of professional evaluators and where possible, avoid them. As a result, few schools are able to produce viable internal or external evaluation programs. Other complaints associated with school evaluation include:

1. It comes too late to do any good.
2. Too few people know how to interpret the results.
3. Evaluation tools are of poor quality.
4. No one validates the evaluation.
5. It is designed to trap teachers for dismissal or non-renewal purposes.
6. Excess time spent evaluating detracts from instruction.

We should all strive to eliminate the above complaints in our schools.

SOME PROMISING ASPECTS OF EVALUATION

If it is true that evaluation in a typical school setting presents problems, it also follows that evaluation is not without a number of pluses. Evaluation has brought about a number of quality improvements in the instructional process. Some evaluation studies have shown that compensatory education programs meet prescribed goals; other evaluation studies indicate that when over emphasis is applied to a specific instructional skill area, students show marked improvement, i.e., reading and math. Particular evaluation areas that have improved the quality of instruction include field testing, program instruction testing, criterion reference testing and improved goal-oriented staff evaluation programs.

It is the recognition of the above pluses and the realization that the public will continue to demand greater verification of school effectiveness that forces schools to proceed in a positive direction toward more promising evaluation programs. Of greater importance is the need to develop evaluation programs that will enhance the teaching-learning process and insure that schools will provide students with valid instructional experiences.

WHAT SHOULD BE EXPECTED OF THE PRINCIPAL

No school evaluation program can be successful unless leadership is provided at the top. As principal, you must set the example for others to follow by acquiring school evaluation expertise. You must design and develop a plan for total staff participation in the evaluation process. To accomplish this task you may wish to seek the assistance of others or delegate major responsibilities to subordinates. However, you cannot remove yourself from an active role until the evaluation program is operable and established goals and objectives have been met.

Your major role should be to outline cooperatively with staff the scope of the evaluation program. Some areas that should be considered are:

1. What is the purpose of the evaluation program? (Goals and objectives)
2. What evaluation terms will be used and how will staff be familiarized with them?
3. What items will receive priority evaluation status and how will they be chosen?
4. Who will be actively involved and what will their responsibilities be?
5. What logistics need to be taken care of?

The question arises: "Should the principal establish goals and objectives as his first order of business, or should he familiarize staff with evaluation terminology and examine a number of possible evaluation items?" This author believes that the whole school evaluation process will take on greater meaning, purpose and become more receptive to staff if they can identify with the basic rudiments of evaluation. The best way to accomplish this procedure is to prepare a sample evaluation-terms definition sheet and an evaluation priority analysis list. These items can be shared with staff at a workshop session and revisions, modifications, additions and deletions encouraged at this time.

   We should, at this point, discuss a number of basic evaluation terms essential to effective school evaluation.

Principal's List of Basic Evaluation Terms

Informal Evaluation	The most common school evaluation process encompassing observation, teacher judgements, conferences, student self-evaluations and others.
Formal Evaluation	A specific evaluation process designed to measure student progress, program success, goal-objective attainment and total school operation efficiency. Usually based on normative criteria.
Goal-Objective Verification	Measurement data which shows the percentage of participants who met goal-objective requirements through designated process activities.
Program Validation	Evidence gathered and reported to show that a program has achieved stated goals. Validation is offered for justification of continued program operation.
School Effectiveness Data	Evaluation results which relate to stated objectives in terms of specific degrees of success.

Internal Evaluation

The in-school evaluation design or model established and carried out by school staff.

External Evaluation

The use of outside evaluation consultants or agencies for the purpose of evaluating school programs or for validating internal evaluations.

Supplemental Evaluation Terms

Directions: For each term listed write your own definition.
Needs Assessment

Discrepancy analysis

Accountability

We all face the problem of trying to decide which areas should be evaluated first. In our schools we establish a priority checklist which is displayed in Figure 1-1.

PRINCIPAL EVALUATION CHECKLIST
Priority Analysis

Directions: When developing your list add any areas you think should be included for evaluation purposes and then rank them one to ten in order of importance.
(1 highest)

1. Class size
2. Leadership
3. School climate
4. Educational facilities
5. Television instruction
6. Tutoring program
7. Pupil movement
8. Building maintenance

9. Vandalism
10. Instructional supervision
11. Lunchroom operation
12. Student attendance
13. Student competency
14. Innovative programs
15. Student needs
16. Community needs
17. Staff needs
18. Support personnel
19. Guidance effectiveness
20. Health services
21. Parent-teacher communications
22. Instructional materials
23. Resource allocations
24. Library media services
25. School discipline
26. Community volunteers
27. Athletics
28. Intramurals
29. Co-curricular activities
30. Staff development program

31. Inservice program
32. School handbook
33. Individualized instruction
34. Progress recording procedures
35. Reporting methods
36. Promotion and retention
37. School goals
38. Curriculum development/revision
39. Testing
40. School morale
41. Extracurricular activities
42. Teacher evaluation
43. Administrator-teacher relations
44. Learning process
45. Learning conditions
46.
47.
48.
49.
50.
Others
1.
2.
3.

Figure 1-1

The evaluation terms definition sheet and the evaluation priority analysis list provide you and your faculty with a common base from which each can communicate as you proceed to develop goals and objectives, programs and evaluation procedures. These areas will be covered in subsequent chapters.

DEFINING THE ESSENTIAL INGREDIENTS OF A GOOD SCHOOL EVALUATION PROGRAM

Schools should pool their collective staff resources and develop a mode of operation that will allow everyone to share and learn the evaluation process together. Thus, the essential ingredients of a successful school evaluation program will encompass the following:

Involvement: All school personnel should be actively involved in the school evaluation program. The greater the involvement, the more interest and understanding of the ongoing process and the role each plays. Provisions should be made to continually inform less actively involved participants.

Identification: All school areas should be identified and ranked in order of priority for evaluation purposes. Needs assessment activities provide the most effective means of identification. Identification data should provide a basis for establishing school goals and objectives.

Planning: Planning activities should center on program development designed to reach stated goals and objectives. The more people that are involved and the greater the number of planning sessions that take place will decrease the overall implementation period.

Implementation: Sequential implementation steps should be evaluated and alternative changes made whenever desired outcomes are not being achieved.

Evaluation: Evaluation plans must be defined initially for each of the above areas before they go into operation, including details for evaluating the effectiveness of the evaluation. Evaluation should be ongoing and should focus on providing data necessary for making or changing decisions.

Revision: Based upon evaluation results of the evaluation process, the program should be updated and improved each year. Cooperative decisions for change should be sought through the involvement process.

Your school should develop a similar statement of essential ingredients for your evaluation programs.

BASIC PRINCIPLES OF EVALUATION

Student progress should be the school's main concern and the evaluation of effective outcomes must center on the growth of the learner in terms of specified accomplishments. James Lewis refers to basic principles of evaluation as it relates to evaluation of student growth.

"Evaluation, as we have previously learned, is an essential part of education. There are several basic principles underlying any evaluation program. These are:

1. It should indicate student growth in terms of the Thought Processes and Derivatives, Attitudinal Objectives and Psycho-Motor Skills. At all times, evaluation should indicate the progress being made toward the achievement of Behavioral Objectives as they relate to the Thought Processes and Derivatives. It should also include provision for the examination of attitude and, possibly, for development of Psycho-Motor skills.

2. It should be closely related to the Behavioral Objectives of the student and teacher. In addition, evaluation should indicate the degree to which the student has been success-

ful in meeting specific goals as outlined in the Behavioral Objectives. It should also indicate whether or not other goals should be sought.

3. It should be a continuous process. No teacher should wait until the end of the Individual Study Unit to evaluate the progress of the student. It should be administered periodically in stages to check progress as the student pursues his learning experience, constituting a checkpoint where, if necessary, additional directions and recommendations may be made.

4. It should be initiated by the use of several strategies to assess student educational growth. A well-rounded and carefully planned evaluation program includes a multitude of evaluative strategies such as the following:

    a. Observing students while they are working to look for boredom, disinterest or frustration. These are early signs which may clue the teacher to the student who may find his assignment too difficult, or may not understand what is expected of him.

    b. Try out a few checkpoint questions from either the Self-Test or Pre-Test.

    c. Confer with the student to carefully probe the extent of his growth.

    d. Collect and examine some of the materials the student has been working on to check his growth.

    e. Confer with any assistants who may be serving as aides to the teacher about the student.

    A point of concern here is that no single evaluation strategy should be considered "best," but all or one should be used at the discretion of the teacher in terms of the individual student who is the subject of the evaluation. However, because of the time a teacher must and should spend working with individual students, the evaluation strategy should not be too time-consuming. If it is at all possible, para-professionals should be employed to assist the teacher in marking only, bearing in mind, however, that it is the teacher's task to make a reasoned evaluation from the grades indicated by the para-professional.

5. The results of the evaluation should be so indicated on the Unit and other records. In any effective individualized program, keeping accurate and careful records is mandatory. Whenever notations as to the progress of the student are made on the Unit, the date of the observation or checkpoint should also be indicated.

6. Students should also be encouraged to evaluate their own progress. As schools become more and more interested in the individualization of instruction, the student will assume an ever-increasing role in his education. One of the student's new roles will be that of evaluator of his own progress. In certain cases, the student will also be permitted to prescribe his next Unit. When individualized instruction is really on the move, students should be permitted to develop and complete their own Unit for study. There are many ways in which students can be come involved in their evaluation."[1]

School evaluation should focus on two areas: learner progress in terms of cognitive, affective and psycho-motor growth and the development of the institution with regard to effective resource development. i.e., space, staff, budget, etc.

FORMULATING EVALUATION PROGRAM OBJECTIVES

The development of a successful school evaluation program precludes that a number of supportive objectives will be established to reach a desired goal. The goal and all objectives should be carefully listed:

---

1. James Lewis, Jr., *Administering the Individualized Instruction Program* (West Nyack, N.Y.: Parker Publishing Co., Inc., 1971), pp. 118–19.

Anyone's School
Anywhere, U.S.A.

School Evaluation Program

Goal: By 1985 we will develop a comprehensive evaluation plan which will provide for internal and external evaluations designed to measure the effectiveness of our instructional program.

Objectives:

To have all school personnel become involved in the evaluation process.

To form sub-goals and objectives for the total school evaluation program.

To identify all aspects of the school operation that need to be evaluated.

To establish a school evaluation team responsible for the total school evaluation program.

To develop evaluation guidelines for each identified area.

To develop a set of evaluation terms and definitions that all school personnel can understand and use.

To design an evaluation model consistent with stated goals and objectives.

To provide pupil progress profiles for the Phase I priority-objectives program.

To establish an evaluation reporting system that all staff can use as a guideline.

Figure 1-2

While this list may not be complete, it does provide a common base direction that all school personnel can identify with and work from, as the evaluation program takes shape.

THE NEED FOR SCHOOL AND DISTRICT ARTICULATION

School evaluation goals and objectives need to be in harmony with district programs. It is desirable for a school to develop a program above and beyond district expectations. The question arises: "How much should our school do independently?" The answer: "As much as is humanly possible to make the school highly effective." The building level is where it all happens and it is here that the question has to be answered: "How effective is this school?"

Evaluation program objectives should be continually examined for consistency and validity. Care must be taken to insure that there are no gaps with other upper or lower grade level schools in the district. If gaps or potential conflicts are evident, then possible solutions should be explored.

Familiarity with what other schools are doing and an understanding of the district program are the responsibility of the principal. You should assume the leadership role necessary for bringing your school from minimum district expectations to an advanced quality program. To accomplish this, it must be assumed that every process that occurs within the scope of the school has a prescribed procedure of operation and a consistent built-in ongoing evaluation process. This is a goal worth striving for! Where possible, nothing should be left to chance. The effectiveness of any school depends on its ability to identify and evaluate its many functions.

SUMMARY

Present school evaluation methods need to be improved, updated and expanded to insure that quality education is offered to all children. School evaluation often presents problems but these are outweighed by the positive aspects of a good evaluation program. The role of the principal in evaluation is one of involvement and leadership.

You, as principal, need to become familiar with evaluation terms, checklists, essential program ingredients, basic principles and program objectives. Your school evaluation program should be articulated and in harmony with district programs.

Needs Assessment: 2
A Key to Accurate Evaluation

Every school and/or district is obligated to investigate its operational status periodically. Are we meeting the needs of children, staff and community? Have we planned for building upkeep, program expansion, space requirements and dozens of other unknown variables? Does the community feel that they are well informed and have a say in our school program? These and numerous other questions need to be formulated and answered.

WHAT DOES YOUR SCHOOL ASSESS?

What is assessed will be dependent on what you, as principal, or the school district administration perceives should be assesed in terms of priorities. You, as a building principal, may feel that your particular building in the district should do a needs assessment based upon school board and district goals.

The assessment may focus on certain specific areas within the total school operation such as inservice, curriculum development or evaluation, or a needs assessment may be all inclusive, designed to cover all operational areas of a school.

An example of a selected specific needs assessment topic might look like this: Specific Topic—Inservice Education (questions)

- Do inservice needs coincide with those of recertification, staff development and staff evaluation?
- Are the workshops conducted in our school designed to meet the needs and interests of the professional staff?
- Do the teachers understand the goals and objectives of the inservice program?
- Does the inservice program offer a wide variety of activities designed to upgrade staff competency skills based upon identified needs?

At the other end of the needs assessment spectrum is the total school community project which could include a number of statements similar to those below:

- Student instruction should center around community work and projects.
- Opportunities for discussion of controversial issues within classroom settings are desirable.
- Specific skills should be mastered by all students before graduation.
- Values taught in school must be consistent with those commonly accepted in this country.

- It is important that students be exposed to the fine arts.
- Our grading and marking procedure is an appropriate indicator of a child's knowledge.
- Environmental education needs to become integrated into the total curriculum.

WHO DOES THE ASSESSMENT?

Actually, two questions need to be answered: Who will be responsible for needs assessment planning and who will be responsible for implementation? In keeping with the *involvement* concept necessary for sound school operation, the representative committee is recommended. The needs assessment committee should represent the total school population to be assessed. The composition of the assessment committee will depend on the nature of the assessment, i.e., one subject area, one school program and/or the total school operation. A total school operation needs assessment committee might consist of the following: parents, students, grade level teachers, administrators, board members and other community groups such as service organizations, P.T.A., senior citizens, etc.

All parties should be represented and given opportunities to provide viable input. It is important that each participant be treated as an equal partner and that the input each provides be given careful consideration when decisions are made. Unless all members are made to feel that they are truly representative, the assessment tool developed will be less than valid.

WRITING THE OPERATIONAL DESCRIPTION

Once the needs assessment committee has been officially designated and a meeting date has been established, you or your designated administrator in charge of the needs assessment should develop an initial operational description. The operational description should attempt to spell out, as briefly and concisely as possible, the goal, objectives, status of the committee and other pertinent data necessary for the group to function effectively.

The purpose of the operational description should be to provide a common base of understanding for all committee members during their organizational period. No attempt should be made to make the document a perfected product; rather, it should be emphasized to the members of the committee that what they have been given is a working draft and that the first order of business might be to add, delete or otherwise revise as needed.

The following is a sample needs assessment committee operational description:

Needs Assessment Committee
Operational Description

Goal:	To identify and develop priority school needs through involvement of staff, students, parents and other community members.
Major Objective:	From a priority list of needs, the school, in cooperation with its district administration, will develop school educational goals, long-range objectives, short-range objectives, and action plans designed to evaluate the quality of goal and objective attainment.
Status:	Members of the needs assessment committee will have the authority to develop and implement a school needs assessment program. The chairman of the committee will serve as liaison to the school principal, who shall serve as an ex officio member. The committee will receive its charge from the principal.

Training: The administration shall conduct a basic skills workshop for committee members. Sufficient guideline materials will be made available for the committee to use in the selection of assessment questions. Several methods of gathering the data will be explored.

Budgetary
Considerations: The needs assessment committee chairman will develop, with the principal, a display of resources needed to hold workshops and meetings, and to implement the assessment.

Membership: Three parents—one chairman
Middle school principal or designee
Other district teacher
Three middle school teachers
Two students
Two non-parent community members
Central office administrator
Board member
Service club member

Meeting Schedule: The needs assessment committee will meet every other Monday from 7:00—8:30 p.m. until such time as the assessment has been implemented, tallied and reported on. It shall be reconvened periodically when necessary to update the original assessment.

Reporting Procedure: The needs assessment commit-
                        tee, through its chairman, will
                        report its findings to the school
                        principal and, if desired, the
                        school   board   through   the
                        Superintendent of Schools.
                        The principal will be responsi-
                        ble for reporting the results to
                        the public.

Miscellaneous: By design, the chairman and at
                        least one other committee
                        member should interpret the
                        data to the principal and the
                        school board when the board
                        follows up the assessment with
                        a development of district goals.

Figure 2-1

DETERMINING WHERE YOU WOULD LIKE TO BE

Too often needs assessments are conducted only to identify
trouble areas or general problems within a particular program or
school. This approach, while providing a means of ascertaining
existing areas that need attention and possible improvement, fails
to provide a mechanism for identifying the ultimate desired program.

Making provisions for isolating "fixits" is a must; however this
method will not insure that community expectations, desires or
needs are being identified and consequently cared for. Thus, any
planned needs assessment should address itself to the question:
Where would we like to be?

Input from those responsible for designing the assessment
model should focus on listing those things most desirable for the
specific area to be assessed. If the total curriculum is to be the assessment area, then a sample listing of topics might include any or
all of the following:

1. Health Education
2. Sex Education
3. Remedial Reading
4. Remedial Math
5. Electives
6. Societal Survival Skills
7. Pre-vocational Courses
8. Vocational Education
9. Career Education
10. Intramurals
11. Study Halls
12. Field Trips
13. Community Education
14. Consumer Education
15. Interdisciplinary Instruction
16. Environmental Education
17. Co-op Work Study
18. Athletics
19. Morals—Values
20. Basic Competency Skills
21. Drug Education
22. Patriotism and Citizenship

It follows that the types of questions to be answered from each area will depend on how the representative assessment group feels about the topic. If several people feel that sex education is missing from the health curriculum or that a health curriculum is lacking, then several questions relative to the subject need to be formulated. In the *should have* or *like to be* category, the following sample questions might be developed:

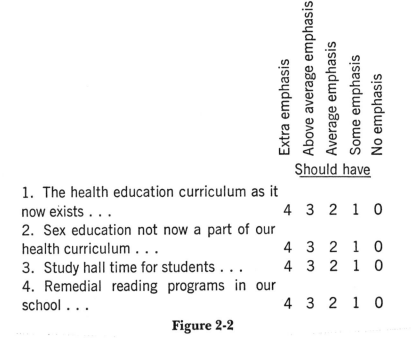

	Extra emphasis	Above average emphasis	Average emphasis	Some emphasis	No emphasis
			Should have		
1. The health education curriculum as it now exists . . .	4	3	2	1	0
2. Sex education not now a part of our health curriculum . . .	4	3	2	1	0
3. Study hall time for students . . .	4	3	2	1	0
4. Remedial reading programs in our school . . .	4	3	2	1	0

Figure 2-2

This procedure may be utilized to assess where you would like to be for all other areas within your school. Example: A needs assessment may be developed to cover facilities, space, building maintenance, renovations, etc. To this point we have only discussed the questionnaire approach to needs assessment. This is not to imply that this is the only method used or the best alternative. Needs assessment methods will be discussed in detail later in this chapter.

The *should have* or *would like to be* approach to needs assessment insures that careful attention will be given to the ultimate in program development. Not all that is identified will be feasible, however, because of staff, facilities, budget and other constraints.

ASCERTAINING WHERE YOU ARE NOW

Two approaches are possible when attempting to find out just where you are now in relation to where you would like to be. The first approach assumes that some representative group, i.e., the assessment committee, board advisory group, the board and administration, or some other body will determine just how close or far away you are from each need identified in the *sould have* assessment. This method can be used effectively if people who are knowledgable and conversant with the school operation are members of the representative group.

A more viable approach is to include within the assessment mechanism itself a *where are we now* component. More specifically, when those who are being assessed respond to what the schools *should have*, they should also respond to what schools *have now*. Just as each question was followed by a *should have* 4–0 rating column in the previous example, so too would it be preceeded by a *have now* 4–0 column. A sample portion of such a list can be seen in Figure 2-3.

When combined, the assessment will provide information that will give an indication of how much discrepancy there is between what people perceive to be in existence and what they feel should be in existence. The Batesville, Arkansas, School District #1 Needs Assessment points this process out in greater detail utilizing a slightly different format, as shown in Figure 2-4.

<u>Schools have now</u>

Extra Emphasis	Above average emphasis	Average emphasis	Some emphasis	No emphasis	
4	3	2	1	0	The health education curriculum as it now exists.
4	3	2	1	0	Sex education not now a part of the health curriculum.
4	3	2	1	0	Study hall time for students.
4	3	2	1	0	Remedial reading programs in our middle schools

Figure 2-3

A Survey of Educational Needs

Batesville School District #1

January, 1976

The following format was used to respond to each item on the questionnaire.

SHOULD EXIST

(0) Do not know the extent to which the condition exists in my school

(1) Condition should not exist at all in my school

(2) Condition should exist to a slight extent

(3) Condition should exist to a moderate extent

(4) Condition should exist to a fairly large extent

ACTUALLY EXISTS

(0) Do not know the extent to which the condition exists in my school

(1) Condition does not exist at all in my school

(2) Condition exists to a slight extent

(3) Condition exists to a moderate extent

(4) Condition exists to a fairly large extent

(5) Condition should exist   (5) Condition exists to a
      to a very large extent   very large extent

EXAMPLE: Should Exist   Actually Exists
The teachers in our school
take an individual interest in
their students   5   3

Figure 2-4

In the example, the person answering has indicated (5) that he believes, to a very large extent, that teachers should take an individual interest in the students, and (3) that he believes, to a moderate extent, that teachers in his school do take an individual interest in their students.

Not all needs assessment has to be done through the use of the written questionnaire. Your school may choose to utilize one or more of the unique approaches offered in the next section.

UNIQUE WAYS TO CONDUCT AN ASSESSMENT

Class Project:

One viable approach to a school needs assessment is the class project identifying a central need goal. Justification for using this type of project rests on the planning and employment of sound student learning experiences.

The central need goal may be to establish the effectiveness of the school in terms of discipline, community expectations, program offerings or other aspects of the school operation. Learning experiences may inculcate such techniques as interviewing, questionnaire development, categorizing, tallying, report writing, large and small committee assignments, panel discussions and numerous other learning experiences depending on the type of assessment methods utilized.

The class project is an excellent learning experience for upper grade level students grades 8-9 in a middle or junior high school and grades 9-12 in a high school. It is possible to conduct an assessment utilizing lower grade levels when the subject to be assessed is scaled down and a greater active role is assumed by the teacher involved.

Class Assessment Project Guidelines
(Sample project)

Activity:	Class school needs assessment
Participants:	Social Studies class—Grade 10 Teacher—Mr. Alboss
Major Goal:	To do an assessment of school discipline needs as seen by students, parents, staff, administrators and other community groups.
Major Objectives:	To involve all students in a class assessment project To determine the disciplinary needs of the school To offer some possible suggestions to meet identified needs To provide students with a variety of skills necessary to carry out a successful assessment

Learning Skills:	Group organizational development skills
	Questionnaire development and use
	Interviewing techniques
	Tallying and summarizing
	Writing reports
	Discrepancy analysis
Procedural Operation:	Hold class discussion on perceived needs.
	List perceived needs developed by class.
	Seek additional perceived needs from parents, other students, staff and administrators.
	Develop a Do Now—Should Do questionnaire.
	Assign questionnaire delivery and return tasks.
	Establish tallying and recording methods.
Reporting process:	The report will be written in its entirety.
	Significant highlights will be noted by asterisk.
	Recommendations will be made when the class deems them appropriate.
	Copies of the report shall be made available to all participants and other interested parties.
Miscellaneous:	Time lines for each operation should be established.

SENAC:

(School Educational Needs Assessment Committee)
This lay committee functions much like a principal's advisory or evaluation committee. It differs in that its

major charge is to discover school needs and their priorities.

The committee can be organized by the principal or any combination of the principal, administrative council or other governing body in the school. Most authorities recommend that a committee of this nature operate for a set period of time and from a specific charge handed down by the principal or his designee.

The major purpose of this committee will be to conduct a school needs assessment within guidelines established by the principal and committee members.

A number of principals have experienced success with the on-going no time-frame committee. The advantage of this approach lies in the ability of the committee to start small and develop some assessment expertise as it progresses. It also allows for specific areas to be assessed, and the committee can spend additional time in developing possible alternative solutions for specified needs.

The ongoing assessment process fosters greater community interaction with school personnel and helps to insure that a continuing needs identification program for the school will remain in effect.

SENAC GUIDELINES

Activity:	Lay citizens' needs assessment.
Participants:	Public members selected by the school.
	Designated school personnel to serve as liaison and resource people to the committee.

Major Goal:	To determine what needs to be done to update the present pupil progress reporting system.
Major Objectives:	To identify existing problems in the reporting systems through questionnaires, interviews, etc.
	To collect existing samples of reporting tools from several other districts to help in the needs identification process.
	To design or modify the present reporting systems based upon derived needs.
Committee Skills:	Assessment methods and techniques.
	Group organization skills.
	Applying discrepancy analysis procedures.
	Reporting.
Procedural Operation:	Organize committee (chairman, clerk, etc.).
	Determine scope of assessment and committee status.
	Establish main assessment methods—alternates, if applicable.
	Develop list of perceived needs for use with assessment tool (questionnaire, interview, etc.).
	Carry out assessment assignments.
	Report results and any recommendations prescribed.
Reporting Process:	Continual dialogue will be established by the committee with the principal.
	A final written report will be submitted to the principal with a copy for the Director of Secondary Education.

	Alternate solutions for meeting identified needs will be listed.
	Recommended solutions will be noted with appropriate rationale.
Miscellaneous:	Develop a list of committee resources needed.
	Other considerations not covered in the above guidelines should be listed.

Principal's Assessment:	The principal, as the designated leader of the school, may provide the initiative for identifying major school needs. Your needs assessment can focus on the total school operation or any specific area identified by you, faculty, and/or parents as being pertinent.
	The most effective approach to a principal's assessment entails your gathering a list of perceived needs from such groups as parents, civic organizations, student representatives and staff.
	After compiling a master list of perceived needs, you can set about having the same groups assign the list priority on a 1–20 basis of importance. Probably the most positive aspect of this method of needs assessment centers on your ability to carry on a face-to-face dialogue with participants. This approach helps to identify you as one who actively participates in improving the effectiveness of the school.

PRINCIPAL'S ASSESSMENT GUIDELINES

Activity: Principal's assessment.

Participants: Principal, parents' group, civic or-
                            ganizations, senior citizens, student
                            representation and school staff.

Major Goal: To provide a detailed school needs as-
                            sessment through personal contact
                            with selected target groups using sev-
                            eral assessment techniques.

Major Objectives: To gather needs data on the total
                            school operation by generalizing 30%
                            of the data to cover all areas.

                            To place a major emphasis on cur-
                            riculum and instruction by designing
                            70% of required responses in this
                            area.

                            To assign priority to identified needs
                            on a rank order basis 1–15 by resub-
                            mitting the iist to the original target
                            groups.

                            To endeavor to resolve the top three
                            needs by priority the first year.

                            To establish a long-range plan to re-
                            solve the remaining items on the 1–15
                            list.

Skills Needed: Questionnaire development.
                            Ability to conduct group sessions.
                            Reporting techniques.

Procedural Operation: Form advisory group to assist in es-
                            tablishing initial list of perceived
                            needs.

                            Conduct first needs assessment.

                            Redo assessment two months later—
                            have groups rank order 1–15.

                            Tally results and develop a
                            standardized reporting format.

	Start process for resolving foremost school needs.
Reporting Process:	A final written report will be submitted to previously designated central office personnel.
	All participants will be offered an opportunity to secure a copy of the report.
	The report will include any proposed solutions to identified needs.
Miscellaneous:	Budgetary and other resource implications should be listed in an appendix.

THE QUESTIONNAIRE AS AN ASSESSMENT TOOL

Most school-needs assessment endeavors start and end with a questionnaire. While often overworked and misused, the questionnaire, when properly utilized within recognized limitations, can be a most formative assessment tool. The questionnaire, when used under established guidelines can be the most effective and practical needs assessment tool available to you.

Guidelines for Quesionnaire Developments

1. The major goals of the questionnaire must be delineated. (Examples)
   A. The goal of this questionnaire is to determine our foremost instructional needs.
   B. A subdivision of this questionnaire will seek to determine disciplinary needs of the school.
2. Develop questions relevant to your school operation.
3. The questionnaire should be divided in major areas of concern.
   A. Discipline
   B. Instruction
   C. Inservice

    D. Administrative

    E. Testing

    F. Others

4. Separate questionnaires must be developed for teachers, parents and others.

5. The design for answering must be simple enough for the reader to comprehend but concise enough to provide sufficient data.

    (Examples)

    A. Yes _____   No _____

    B. High   1 2 3 4 5   Low

    C. Almost always _____ Usually _____ Sometimes _____ Seldom _____ Never _____

6. List those responsible for the development of the questionnaire.

7. Devise a means for a tryout phase.

    A. Check for problems with the questionnaire as an instrument by having different groups of people fill it out.

    B. Revise the questionnaire when necessary.

Methods of Questionnaire Use

1. Mail to all parents and other community members.

    A. Self-addressed and stamped envelope

    B. Allow parents or their children to return it

    C. Other

2. Utilize a staff meeting for teachers' questionnaire.

3. Select homeroom or other non-academic time for students to fill out student questionnaire.

4. Utilize administrative council or other established time for administrators to answer their form.

Tabulating the Questionnaire

1. Decide on persons responsible for tabulation.

2. Develop a standardized method of tabulation—spell out how it is to be done.

3. Determine procedure to be utilized for recording tabulated results.

4. Develop a cross-check system to insure accuracy of first tabulation.

Reporting the Questionnaire Data

1. Who is to do the reporting?
2. Who will be responsible for receiving the report? (Decision maker)
3. How will it be presented? Written, oral, visual, etc.
4. Are conclusions or other analytical contents to be included?
5. Will the report be made public? If so, through what media?

Developing A Needs List From the Questionnaire Report

1. List all apparent needs by major areas of concern.
   Example: (curriculum, discipline, record keeping, communications, etc.)
2. Assign priority to each item on the list.
3. Reorder list into three categories:
   A. Those that can be changed, utilizing present school resources.
   B. Those that may be changed if additional resources can be procured.
   C. Those that call for resources unlikely to be available in the future.

It is essential that needs having absolutely no chance of being met because of existing and/or anticipated future conditions be excluded from the list. Time, effort, energy and money can be saved if decision makers recognize and select only those needs that the school can realistically meet through the change process.

Sample Questionnaire Categories

			Yes	No
Discipline	Student	Teachers establish classroom discipline early and are more effective teachers as a result.	_____	_____
	Parent	Classroom discipline is established by teachers early in the year.	_____	_____
	Teacher	A teacher needs to establish discipline early to be effective.	_____	_____
	Administrator	The vast majority of teachers establish discipline in their classrooms early in the year.	_____	_____

			High Low
Instruction	Student	Individualized instruction taking the needs of each student into consideration is practiced by teachers.	1 2 3 4 5
	Parent	Children are taught based upon recognized individual needs.	1 2 3 4 5
	Teacher	The individualized instruction approach based on childrens' needs in my classroom rates	1 2 3 4 5
	Administrator	Individualized instruction based on recognized individual needs rates	1 2 3 4 5

		Always	Most Often	Usually	Occasionally	Rarely ever
Student	The school administration is supportive of new programs and activities teachers wish to try.	—	—	—	—	—
Parent	Administrators readily lend support to teachers' ideas for new programs and activities.	—	—	—	—	—
Teacher	I have the support of the administration when suggesting new programs and activities.	—	—	—	—	—
Administrator	I support and encourage teachers to try out new programs and activities.	—	—	—	—	—

Administrative Support (label at left side)

Figure 2-5

ADDITIONAL ASSESSMENT TOOLS

The questionnaire continues to be the most popular and perhaps the most effective assessment tool available to any principal; yet, other approaches can be used with considerable success. Following are three that may be used with great success.

Interview

A random sampling interview of the community, staff, students and others can be developed as an alternate assessment tool. The interview can be conducted in person or over the telephone. Two approaches may be utilized:

   1. A series of should have-have now specific questions may be asked and responses recorded without concern for

further need identification. (See example presented earlier in the chapter.)

2. The interviewer may ask the respondent to list five major needs of the school. The interviewer then gives two examples: Stop smoking and provide better food. The respondent then lists five which might look like this:

    A. Better transportation
    B. More discipline
    C. New report cards
    D. More homework
    E. A new principal

The interviewer then proceeds to establish specific perceived needs by following up the responses with additional inquiry on each answer listed.

Example: *Question*

What part of the transportation operation do you feel needs improvement?

Response

Busing students so early in the morning. My children get the bus at 7:00 a.m. It's too early and they have to wait at school an hour before they start classes. They're not doing well in school because they get tired in the afternoon.

A specific transportation need has been identified and should be listed. The number of times other interviewers and respondents identify this as a need should be recorded. This procedure will help to rank order identified needs.

Radio Call-In

The radio call-in is a tool that can be of particular value to a small community with one high school, middle school or junior high school. Arrangement can be made with the local radio show to conduct such a program with you or the assessment committee designated as the recipient of the calls. Radio personnel can initiate a discussion on school needs and invite calls from individuals to express their impressions.

It is essential that appropriate planning for advanced publicity take place. Notices can be sent home from school announcing the show, and the radio station can publicize the special public service program regularly during the preceding week.

Ground rules should be established so that the show doesn't turn into a "gripe" session. People calling in should politely be instructed to state a need for improvement. You or a member of the committee should then ask further questions, if desired, similar to the example found in the interview section.

Community Coffee Hour

You can hold planned periodic coffee hours at the school for the purpose of inviting community members in to discuss their need perceptions. Invitations may be sent out to parents, one grade level for each session, and additional invitations to attend may be extended to community members at large through the news media.

Perceived needs can be discussed and a priority ranking of needs established at each session. A compilation of all needs from each session should be developed and a written report published, listing the highest priority needs. The report should include, if possible, any proposed plans developed to resolve identified needs. The school newsletter and the local news media serve as excellent reporting vehicles. Follow-up coffee hours often provide an excellent means of personalizing the reporting process.

UTILIZING YOUR NEEDS DATA FOR EVALUATION PURPOSES

Needs data collected, collated and reported should be analyzed for validation purposes. We should establish a procedure which will identify needs that are perceived and those that are real and in need of futher action. How does one determine which needs are valid? The following criteria should be utilized to establish those needs that require further action.

1. Rank order needs from the highest to lowest frequency of occurrence.

2. Re-examine the first five within the school setting and re-establish the order of priority based on any additional information gathered.

3. Based upon resources available to the school, determine where need areas change can take place.

4. Discard those needs where no change can occur because of unavailable resources.

5. Develop a procedure for establishing action-plan goals designed to meet selected needs.

PLANNING FOR REASSESSMENT ACTIVITIES

You have completed your needs assessment—when should you plan for the next one? As a guideline, schools should have a general total school operation assessment every three years and specific area assessments periodically as needed.

The results of the evaluation program you develop to measure the success of your action plan will help to determine the frequency of specific area assessments. The appointment of an ongoing faculty-parent-student needs assessment committee for the purpose of future assessment planning is a viable approach.

Needs assessment is a necessary prerequisite to evaluation—it should not be a one shot program.

SUMMARY

Needs assessment is an essential part of any successful school evaluation program. Initially, it is important to determine what you wish to assess and then proceed to write an operational description to tell how you will go about it. The major goal of the needs assessment should be to determine where you are now in relation to where you would like to be. Once this has been accomplished, programs may be developed to meet determined needs.

The needs assessment questionnaire is the most effective tool to use but not the only one available. Additional assessment tools include interviews, radio call-ins and coffee hours. Methods need to be established for proper use of needs data and plans should be formulated for ongoing reassessment activities.

Evaluating

3

School Goals and Objectives

A sound needs assessment program precludes that a measure of accuracy will prevail when a school establishes its priority goals based upon assessment data. Meaningful evaluation has to be congruent with goal development. You will find that without goal statements there can be no measure of accomplishment and/or success.

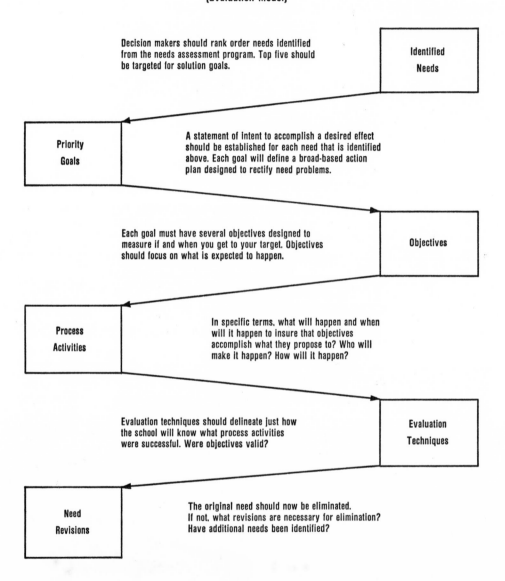

SCHOOL GOALS AND OBJECTIVES
(Evaluation Model)

Decision makers should rank order needs identified
from the needs assessment program. Top five should
be targeted for solution goals.

Identified
Needs

Priority
Goals

A statement of intent to accomplish a desired effect
should be established for each need that is identified
above. Each goal will define a broad-based action
plan designed to rectify need problems.

Each goal must have several objectives designed to
measure if and when you get to your target. Objectives
should focus on what is expected to happen.

Objectives

Process
Activities

In specific terms, what will happen and when
will it happen to insure that objectives
accomplish what they propose to? Who will
make it happen? How will it happen?

Evaluation techniques should delineate just how
the school will know what process activities
were successful. Were objectives valid?

Evaluation
Techniques

Need
Revisions

The original need should now be eliminated.
If not, what revisions are necessary for elimination?
Have additional needs been identified?

Figure 3-1

NEEDS ASSESSMENT AND GOAL RELATIONSHIPS

Once the needs assessment has revealed the most pressing needs of your school, a sequential pattern for total school operation should evolve:

- School goal preparation must bear a direct relationship to priority need statements.
- Objectives should be designed to reach goals.
- Program development must be in direct harmony to goal-objective activity.
- Evaluation plans must reflect objectivity, validity and utility in making the school a more effective place for students to learn.

With needs data and goal statements in congruence, your school may proceed with the selection of appropriate learning experiences designed to make goal statements a reality. Inherent in this action is the need to create measurable objectives and follow through with process activities which spell out specifically how objectives will be met.

The school goal and objectives (evaluation model) outlines the desired sequence.

SCHOOL GOALS AND OBJECTIVES—EVALUATION MODEL

(Sample Application)

Priority Need #1: The need to expand the teaching of basic reading skills in an effort to bring all students up to grade level.

Goal Statement: To increase the number of students reading at grade level by June 15.

OBJECTIVES

To increase the amount of reading instruction time during the school day.	To expand the Right to Read program so that more students will be included.

To insure that remedial reading programs are articulated by grade levels.

To update teachers on reading instruction techniques.

To have 90% of our students reading on grade level by June 15.

PROCESS ACTIVITIES

Each teacher will develop a plan to add five additional minutes a day of reading-related instruction for each class.

The Right to Read Program will be expanded in September by adding $500.00 and the number of volunteers doubled.

The reading committee this summer will undertake a study of the remedial program and make recommendations based on their findings

A series of three workshops designed to improve teacher effectiveness will be run in the fall by the reading committee.

Grade level tests will be developed by the evaluation group to measure student grade level ability.

EVALUATION TECHNIQUES

All teacher plans for additional reading related instruction will be submitted to the reading committee in September for review. The committee will make suggestions where appropriate.

A check will be made by the principal periodically to see that the money is spent on Right to Read and that the volunteer corps is doubled.

A committee will work this summer to evaluate where, if any, gaps exist in our sequential instruction pattern

An evaluation sheet will be developed for each workshop sessions and participants will be asked to submit their evaluations.

The Gates-McGinty Reading Tests will be readministered to all students in June. Other tests will be developed as needed.

NEED REVISIONS
(Fill in when evaluation data is complete.)

1.

2.

3.

Figure 3-2

THE PRINCIPAL'S ROLE IN GOAL
SELECTION AND
EVALUATION

You or your designee determines whether an effective school goal selection and evaluation program becomes a reality. If support and initiative is not forthcoming from the top, the overall effectiveness of any school will remain an unknown. Ideally you should involve teachers and other administrators in the process, but ultimately you must actively support and participate in the program.

The selection of school goals may take place in three ways. The first and least productive occurs when goals are decreed from the school board or central office to the principal. Second, the principal as the instructional leader of the school may initiate certain goals. This is a commendable approach when the principal offers his goals as suggestions or possibilities for staff consideration. Third, the staff may initiate suggestions or request certain goals for the principal's consideration. This approach should be encouraged and a special procedure established to make it a reality. Ideally, a combination of the second and third approaches should be developed to insure maximum staff involvement, input, and participation in the goal implementation process.

As principal you assume the major responsibility for determining to what degree school goals have been met. Once the degree of success has been established, a progress report should be developed and sent to appropriate parties. Specifically, this information should be made available to teachers, parents, central office staff and other interested parties.

Eastern Junior High School in Riverside, Connecticut, under the direction of Principal Benjamin Davenport, has been in the forefront of this type of evaluation report. The following is a sample of Mr. Davenport's goal evaluation report to central office staff:

GREENWICH PUBLIC SCHOOLS

Eastern Junior High School

51 Hendrie Avenue

Riverside, Connecticut 06878

(203) 637-1744

Benjamin Davenport
  Principal
A. Miles Weaver
Assistant Principal

TO: DR. WILFRED WOLFFER   DATE: MAY 1, 19XX
     MR. ATWELL BOOKMILLER
FROM: BENJAMIN DAVENPORT
SUBJECT: FINAL REPORT RE: MANAGEMENT EVALUA-
TION

I. GOAL—To insure communication with Eastern's many
   communities.
   PROCESS OBJECTIVES
   1. *Insure thirty percent of students and parents meet
      with their guidance counselors regarding school pro-
      gress.* Thirty-two percent of the student body had a
      meeting with their guidance counselor and parents be-
      tween September and March of the 19XX–XY school
      year. Evening appointments were held by counselors
      to facilitate parent conferences. Thirty-two percent
      does not include parent conferences via telephone
      which account for an additional twenty-six percent.
   2. *Insure five informative newsletters are sent to parents.*
      We have doubled the size of the newsletters, and have
      had five newsletters. (Appendix 1)
   3. *Insure program team functions and the school
      evaluates the objectives for the current year and writes
      objectives for the following year.* The program team is

functioning well and evaluation and objectives will be ready on schedule. (Appendix 2)

4. *Print and distribute to the public school goals and objectives for current year and evaluation of school goals and objectives for preceding year.* This has been completed. (Appendix 3)

5. *Insure small group parent coffees take place and feedback is given to school personnel and parents.* Fifteen small group coffees were held at Eastern between September 22 and October 15. All staff, superintendents, directors, coordinators, and secondary principals were given a summary of questions asked at the parent coffees. The summary was also printed in the November issue of the Eastern Chatter. (Appendix 4)

6. *Insure the school has two open houses for parents.* Two open houses were held, one for the 7th grade, September 11th, and one for the 8th and 9th grades on September 30th.

7. *Insure the school sends out Christmas cards to all volunteers and parents who have been friends of the school.* Over 150 Christmas cards were sent to friends of Eastern. (The Christmas card was designed by students.)

8. *Insure Eastern publicity in town newspapers.* Eastern has had many articles printed in the Greenwich Time and has had a weekly article printed in the Old Greenwich Gazette. The number of articles printed in the town's newspapers have increased by approximately 35% over last year.

II. GOAL—Insure Alternative Learning Programs for Eastern are studied.
PROCESS OBJECTIVES

1. *Insure school has a definition of alternative learning.* After a great deal of faculty dialogue, all staff members were given a definition of alternative learning on October 14. (Appendixes 5 & 6)

2. *Discuss alternative learning with Program Team, Fa-*

culty Senate, Curriculum Committee, PTA, and Principal's Board. This has been accomplished and is continuing with the Program Team and Faculty Senate.

3. *Have administrative team and Senior Teachers discuss alternative learning.* This was completed and all Senior Teachers and Teacher Leaders turned in reports regarding alternatives during the month of September.

4. *Have Inservice Day devoted to alternative learning.* The entire Inservice Day in October was devoted to alternative learning.

5. *Insure needs assessment in regard to alternative learning takes place and a report is written.* Each department did a needs assessment and a report has been written.

6. *Insure Program Team and Eastern administration study alternative needs assessment in regard to future curriculum development.* The administration and the Program Team are presently involved in a needs assessment of the school. (Appendixes 7 & 8)

Figure 3-3

ESTABLISHING GOALS AND OBJECTIVES WITH STAFF

The preface section of this book stated: "Successful evaluation programs are predicated on close collaboration among school partners . . . " Nowhere is this concept more crucial than in defining school goals and objectives on a basis of priority. The *involvement* of school staff in the development, implementation and evaluation of school goals and objectives must occur before any school can expect to be highly effective.

It is the school staff who must insure, through their participation in the day-to-day operation of the teaching-learning process, that cooperatively derived goals and objectives become a reality. To do this, staff must help the principal search for realistic approaches to goal-objective development. Several approaches can be taken to insure staff involvement:

1. A representative staff committee may be appointed or the teaching staff may be asked to choose their own representatives.

2. Total faculty sessions may be held specifically for the purpose of identifying school goals and objectives.

3. A questionnaire sent to all staff members may provide the necessary goal-objective information for the committee or the principal to select goals and objectives by rank order.

When properly conducted, Number 2 should be the most productive approach. In this approach, you as principal, must assume a strong leadership role to insure that staff members understand what their jobs entail and how to perform them effectively. Wherever possible, preliminary materials should be delivered to staff members well in advance of the scheduled meeting. The preliminary materials should include, when possible, descriptive samples and examples of the work expected and suggested instructions for accomplishing the task at hand. The following are offered as examples of this method:

Inservice–September 26

Hopeville Junior High—Afternoon Session
Topic: Building Level Goals and Objectives

Attached hereto is a copy of goals established by another junior high school. These may serve as examples, ideas, etc., for similar types to be developed for Hopeville Junior High.

I would suggest that we start out slowly and consider three goals per grade level, i.e., 6, 7, or 8, and three or four for the total school operation.

Procedure: Meet first by grade levels for 45 minutes. Develop three goals and process objectives (designed to reach goals).

Example 1: Develop a plan for a modified self-contained/departmentalized program for Grade 6 by May 15.
Objectives to accomplish same
1.
2.
3.
4.

Example 2: To create a better student grouping distribution more conducive to individualized instruction for grades 7 and 8.
Objectives to accomplish same
1.
2.
3.
4.

Procedure: (cont.)
Meet by total faculty. List a number of goals the school should attempt to accomplish for the rest of the year.

Evaluate these goals until you have identified the priority of the top three.

Develop process objectives designed to meet those goals by June. In establishing process objectives give some thought to who, when, where, how, etc.

That which is left undone can be put on a future faculty agenda.

Figure 3-4

Another list of cooperatively designed objectives from Eastern Junior High School in Riverside, Connecticut, follows:

EASTERN JUNIOR HIGH SCHOOL

Intellectual Skills: (1 area of 6)

1. Eighty percent of the students in grades 7, 8, and 9 will achieve at their individual expectancy level in the basic skills of mathematics and reading as measured by the results of standardized achievement tests.

2. Eighty percent of the students will achieve at their expectancy level as measured by their report card grades in regular learning programs.

3. Maintain the present alternative learning opportunities for students as measured by administrative and departmental reports.

4. Students who are gifted and talented by national standards will be recognized and a special program will be devised to insure that these students are challenged in grades 7, 8, and 9. Evaluation will be measured by special programs operating in all three grades.

5. To insure the "whole child" is not overlooked in the educational process, increased interdisciplinary cooperation and study will take place. Evaluation will be measured by the number of increased activities between departments.

6. Increase the utilization of the Nature Center. Evaluate by departmental usage reports comparing the current year to previous year.

7. Provide alternate instructional patterns to meet student needs, measured by the number of patterns used in each discipline.

8. Improve the basic skills in mathematics and language arts measured by a decrease in the number of students functioning below grade level in these subjects on the SATs.

9. Insure basic skills are being taught in reading and math to those students who need it most, measured by the functioning of a special reading/math program.

10. A representative group of students, parents, and staff in each program area will design a program of challenging learning experiences based on student interest and ability with at least eighty percent of the students in each program area participating in at *least* one challenging learning experience during the school year as measured from teacher records. Definition of challenging learning experiences: Those educational experiences in addition to the stated curriculum that are designed to challenge and extend all students intellectually.

The principal and his staff should examine and classify goals by categories. Typically, goals fall into three categories:

1. Actual goals written and in operation.

2. Those goals perceived to be school goals but not formalized.

3. Those goals that can be recognized as emerging and in need of further examination in the future.

All goals should be discussed and written out on a display chart similar to Figure 3-5.

Goal Development Worksheet
(Sample)

Actual	Perceived	Emerging
1. Developed a co-ordinating team	1. Better school-community relations	1. Developing a school evaluation model
2. Improving discipline	2. Improved basic competency skills	2. Redefining school operational procedures
3. Upgrading reading program	3. Upgrading inservice program	3. ?
4. Revising reporting practices	4. Adopting new staff evaluation procedures	4. ?
5. Upgrading basic skills	5. ?	5. ?

Figure 3-5

The procedure described in Figure 3-5 allows the administration and staff to work from a common base and is a simple way of keeping track of goals as they are discussed. Further work is necessary to identify those school goals that are consistent or inconsistent with school district goals. It is imperative that you as principal, and your staff not develop goals that are in conflict with or cannot be articulated with district goals. One approach to evaluating the comparability of school goals and district goals is the use of a goal comparability and status chart, an example of which is seen in Figure 3-6.

THE PRINCIPAL DEFINES HIS OBJECTIVES

When you and your staff have cooperatively defined and selected a priority-list of school goals and objectives, you must determine your own objectives for the school year. The following criteria should be adhered to when developing yearly objectives:

1. Objectives should be consistent with designated school objectives.
2. Objectives should not be in conflict wih district priorities.
3. Objectives must be reasonable and attainable.
4. Objectives should meet professional building level and district needs with respect to performance expectations for each area.
5. Objectives must be written in measurable terms.
6. Evaluation procedures should be outlined.

You need not go through an elaborate process or create a voluminous document to state your objectives. The one-page format shown in Figure 3-7 has been used in Sarasota, Florida.

HARTFORD SCHOOL DISTRICT—SCHOOL AND DISTRICT GOALS COMPARABILITY CHART

School Goal Statement	Comparability with District	Goal Evaluation Status			
		Development Stage	In Operation	Revision Process	Success High-Low 1-10
To increase the number of students reading at grade level by June 15	Yes—District Goal #4	Process objectives will be implemented September 1	Heart program only	Heart program to be revised	—
To improve the school discipline program	No goal stated. No conflict indicated	Committee will be formed in September	—	—	—
To revise the student progress reporting system to parents	Yes—District Goal #6		First year completed	Minor changes recommended	8
To design a more comprehensive co-curricular activities program	No goal stated. Possible philosophy conflict?	Pilot program ninth grade in September	—	—	—

Figure 3-6

Principal _____
School _____

Principal's Objectives For The School Year (i.e., his/her own "Job Targets")

Listed below are the objectives, written in measurable terms as identified by the school principal, upon which *his/her own evaluation* for the 19XX-XY school year will be based. These objectives or "Job Targets" have been reviewed and approved by the Associate Superintendent for Instruction.

Personal/Professional "Job Targets" for 19XX-XY:

Building Level "Job Targets" for 19XX-XY:

District-wide "Job Targets" for 19XX-XY:

(Attach additional pages as needed)

Assoc. Supt.'s Signature _____ Date _____
Principal's Signature: _____ Date _____

Figure 3-7

Once defined, you should share your objectives with the total faculty. This process completes the development of school goals and objectives for any given year and allows faculty and administration to work from a common base. The next step in the overall picture requires measurable process objectives to be developed to insure that stated goals will be met.

CREATING MEASURABLE PROCESS OBJECTIVES

Schools frequently pay insufficient attention to the development of the process by which stated objectives will be accomplished. This author visited a number of schools recently and found goals and objectives stated adequately but process activities were often missing. One principal commented, "Our biggest problem this year was our failure to define in specific terms what was supposed to happen and teachers were not quite sure who was responsible for what!"

Thus, the process activity should state who (the coordinating committee) will offer, what (a series of workshops), when (starting the first week in September) and how (all teachers, grades 9 through 12) staff will meet on Monday afternoons.

In the above example, we have spelled out the process which will occur in order to achieve a previously stated objective. When school objectives are not met, the process activities should be evaluated to determine what needs to be upgraded, revised, modified, etc.

DEVELOPING THE EVALUATION TIME FRAME

Priority status should be given to the development of an evaluation sequence designed to measure ongoing progress. The ability to evaluate goal and objective development allows for recycling based upon evaluation findings. It is much more effective to redesign certain goals and objectives when they fail to produce desired effects than it is to advance forward in hopes that subsequent steps will rectify the situation.

The evaluation time-frame allows the school to identify specific time frames when expected actions will enter into the picture. It is important to emphasize that few, if any, goal-objective time-frames will be adhered to. Most effective schools have to readjust time-frames several times before evaluation verifies successful goal attainment. A typical evaluation time-frame might look like this:

Evaluation Time Frame

Instructional Objective Based Program

(Overview)

Needs Assessment #1	September
Objective Development and Acceptance	November
Implementation of Planned Instructional Objectives	
1. Articulate instructional-objectives priorities	December
2. Develop mechanisms for evaluating program	December
A. Priority-objectives	
3. Develop accelerated skill objectives	February
4. Draw up preliminary plan for development of enrichment objectives	March
5. Establish recording and reporting continual progress procedures (Math-Reading)	March
6. Evaluate accelerated skill objectives	June
7. Conduct evaluation of instructional objective program developed to date	
8. Develop rationale for proposed change based on evaluation data	July
9. Present to total faculty new changes recommended for adoption	September
10. Develop revised evaluation time frame	October

Figure 3-8

Needs Assessment #1   September
Objective Development   November
and Acceptance

Monthly Time Frame

Sequential Developments	Dec.	Jan.	Feb.	Mar.	Apr.	May	June	July	Aug.	Sept.	Oct.	Nov.
Articulate Priority Instruction Objectives	│											
Develop Mechanisms for Evaluating Program	│											
Develop Accelerated Objectives			│									
Draw Up Preliminary Plan for Enrichment Objectives				│								
Establish Recording and Reporting Continual Progress Procedures				│								
Evaluate Accelerated Skill Objectives							│					
Conduct Evaluation of Total Program to Date							│					
Develop Rationale for Proposed Changes								│				
Present New Recommendations to Faculty										│		
Develop Revised Evaluation Time-Frame											│	
Additions ?												

──────── Denotes approximate time of month activity will take place

Figure 3-9

REPORTING GOAL EVALUATION RESULTS

Progress reports should be issued to parents, staff, students, advisory groups and the community periodically when applicable. When goals are developed for a year, an end-of-the-year report should be developed by the principal and/or a designated committee.

The goal evaluation report should be brief but concise and should not be weighted with fancy educational jargon. Important ingredients of the evaluation report include:

1. A listing of the general goal area.
2. A statement of the goal.
3. Specific objective(s) designed to reach goal.
4. An evaluation report referring to the objective.
5. Any appropriate recommendations.

Following is a sample year end goal report your school might use as a guideline in developing its own report.

HARTFORD MEMORIAL MIDDLE SCHOOL

White River Jct., Vermont

19XX-XY Goal Evaluation Report

July, 19XY

(Partial sample—2 of 8 areas)

ACADEMIC SKILLS—MATH—GRADE 8—To help each student to fulfill his or her potential in Math.
Objective:

    1. Seventy-five percent of students in grade 8 will complete the Minimum Behavioral Objectives as set forth in the eighth grade math program. The White River Math Test and individual teacher evaluation recorded on pupil profile charts will be used to validate results.

Evaluation Report:

A comparison of the 19XX and 19XY White River Math Test and profile charts indicates that seventy-one percent in 19XX and seventy-nine percent in 19XY completed the Minimum Objectives for eighth grade math.

Objective:

The extent of accelerated learning experiences for those who have mastered Minimum Objectives will be reviewed by math teachers and recommendations for needed alternatives will be made.

Evaluation Report:

The review of Accelerated Learning experiences showed that the school does not offer stimulating and demanding experiences for its students. The following recommendations were made:

A. There should be a closer coordination of both Accelerated and Remedial Programs.

B. There should be a periodic review of those students in Accelerated and Remedial Programs to insure the accuracy of their placement, as well as assessing more closely those students who should be placed in respective programs.

STUDENT ATTITUDES—Develop positive student attitudes toward Memorial Middle School.

Objective—School-wide

1. One hundred percent of the student population will be oriented in positive interpersonal relation techniques so as to better understand the nature of positive self-image.

Evaluation Report:

Using a system of points awarded by students to other students for improving relationships with one another, some ninety percent of 5th and 6th graders and sixty percent of 7th and 8th graders participated in this project.

2. Ninety percent of all 7th and 8th graders will successfully participate in the Activity and Elective Program in such a way as to acquire the minimum Skills/Objectives of the offering.

Evaluation Report:
Only seventy-five percent of the students in grades 7
and 8 actually demonstrated a worthwhile experience
from the Activities and Electives. This data was the result of subjective judgments by the teachers who ran
the offerings.

Figure 3-10

REVISING SCHOOL GOALS AND OBJECTIVES
BASED ON EVALUATION DATA

Hopefully, school goals will be formulated that are attainable,
based upon the school's available resources. Goals that are realistic
and within reach of a school's ability and desire to obtain will be
less likely subject to revisions. However, as the pressure and demands for greater accountability increase, schools may attempt to
pursue goals that go beyond their ability to be met. Evaluation and
the ability to utilize evaluation data for the purpose of selecting
and revising school goals will be an area of expertise required of
all professional school staffs in the future.

Greater emphasis will need to be put on accurately forecast-
ing the effectiveness of school goals and how to utilize evaluation
results to change directions when necessary. Most successful
school goal revisions occur when alternative goal patterns have
been developed based on "what ifs." If _____ happens, we will
switch to alternative goal number 2, etc.

Goal revision should take place when and if evaluation data
indicates that the revision will produce better results than the original goal. In order to make this decision, you, as principal, and
your staff must work toward improved evaluation procedures.
Each goal-objective sequence wil have to be evaluated in order to
revise or modify actual progress patterns. Individuals will have to
develop new or improved evaluation skills and techniques. School
evaluation plans will have to reflect an understanding of the need
for ongoing evaluation.

SUMMARY

School goal preparation must bear a direct relationship to priority needs, and the evaluation program should be designed to measure how well that relationship exists. Your leadership role in goal selection and evaluation is a critical one; however, the success of the total program depends on how well you involve staff in the total process.

School goals must be evaluated to insure that they are not in conflict with or cannot be articulated with district goals. You must define your own goals and objectives and these must be reasonable, attainable and in harmony with building level-district needs.

Once goals and objectives have been adopted, process activities need to be established and carried out to insure success. Written procedures for developing an evaluation time frame and reporting goal evaluation results are essential. School goals and objectives need to be continually revised, based on evaluation data.

School Program 4

Planning and Evaluation

For purposes of definition, we shall refer to program planning as, "The development of modes of operation designed to reach recognized outcome desires based upon previously conducted needs assessment." Reduced to its practical components, it consists of carefully planned instructional activities backed by sufficient support services and other resources necessary to reach previously stated goals.

HOW TO EVALUATE THE SCHOOL PLANNING PROCESS

Before a school can evaluate programs, it must make an effort to evaluate the process it utilizes to plan its program. Do we have a standard operating procedure? Is everyone familiar with the process? Where are we now? Where are we going with program planning? Who? When? How? These and a number of other questions should be answered before serious program development and evaluation can proceed with any validity. The following questions suggest some conditions recommended for evaluating the school planning process:

- Is there a program planning group operating in the school?
- Is this group representative of the parties to be served by the planned program?
- Are provisions made for other people to be actively involved?
- Are there established procedures to *identify* program needs?
- Is sufficient time allotted for program planning so that implementation runs smoothly?
- Does the planning group have adequate resources to operate successfully?
- Does the administration provide necessary leadership and support?

These questions help to evaluate the status of the school program planning operation and to set the stage for developing or reorganizing a program planning team.

THE PROGRAM PLANNING GROUP

This author believes that a successful school is one that epitomizes the theme of involvement. The program planning process needs to insure that all parties who have an interest in the school program play a participatory role or are represented by a parity group when avenues for total participation are limited. The makeup, tasks, and the methods of planning of any group will undoubtedly differ in proportion to the uniqueness of each school. Initially, the principal should assume the temporary role of chairman to get the committee underway.

A well-organized planning group established with appropriate goals and objectives sets the initial stage for insuring that sound program evaluation will take place. A typical planning group model might look like this:

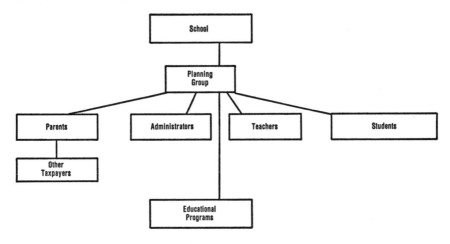

Figure 4-1

The program team at Eastern Junior High School represents one type of involvement process with additional emphasis on an evaluation role also.

Eastern Junior High Program Team

Philosophy

Each year a program team of members representing the entire Eastern Junior High Community—administrators, teachers, parents and students—will meet to propose school goals and objectives for the forthcoming year. It is assumed that the school is properly managed, that school programs are functioning well, that teachers are effectively involved in the learning experience and that parents and students feel good about their school. However, the process of self-evaluation recognizes that the school is constantly seeking improvement. The process is not meant to change the character of the school, but rather to identify areas which need special emphasis during the year or over a period of years in order to accomplish specific outcomes.

This author recommends separate program planning and evaluation teams in each school with established liaison provisions between the two groups. This does not preclude that one group cannot perform both functions, as Eastern has successfully shown over the years.

Initial planning for any instructional-based program should begin with the program team. The approach used will vary, depending on the size of the school and the structure of the program team.

The foremost goal of the program team should be to establish a plan which will detail steps for involving all staff members in formulating any program they will be asked to implement and evaluate.

The following is offered as a sample plan:

Everyone's School
Anywhere, U.S.A.

PLANNING TEAM

Project 1: Spelling Improvement Program
Goal: To develop a complete middle school 5-8 spelling improvement program for all children.

Major
Objective: To provide actual involvement experiences for as many administrators, teachers and parents as is possible and to allow for additional input from those not actually participating. (Student representation will be planned for.)

Procedure: The program team will develop a question and answer flyer which will help provide an overview of the total program for all staff.

Starting in September, the principal will conduct a series of work sessions with staff for the express purpose of planning preliminary basic spelling improvement objectives.

In December, this school will send representatives to meet by grade level and subject area to work out district objectives. Representatives will continue to seek staff input for future meetings.

By February, our school will have its representatives meet with Grade 9 teachers for the purpose of discussing, revising and modifying basic spelling skill objectives Grades 5-9. This group will be responsible for submitting an articulated set of spelling skill improvement objectives to the principal's office on or before June 1.

The principal's office shall be responsible for selecting a representative summer staff group to put the finishing touches on the program. This group will be responsible for insuring that there is continuity at each grade level. They will also develop a profile recording chart to plot the progress of each student.

The completed spelling improvement skill objective program will be reviewed and evaluated with staff during the September orientation sessions. Implementation will begin with the start of school in September.

Periodic progress evaluation by the evaluation team will be held every two months and revisions will be made as deemed necessary.

Publicity: A plan for effective program publicity among the professional staff is a must. A monthly review of progress together with any projected changes will be published and delivered to all staff.

Program development and evaluation reports will be featured in the school newsletter published quarterly. Additional progress reports and instruction sheets to parents will be sent home monthly.

Local newspapers and radio stations will be given periodic news releases and special articles for media coverage will be developed yearly.

A special slide-tape program will be developed to explain the program to local organizations such as the Lions, Rotary, Senior Citizens, Chamber of Commerce and others.

Evaluation: The school evaluation team will develop a sub-evaluation model designed to offer opportunities for all professional staff to participate in the evaluation process.

Evaluation shall be ongoing with a major emphasis on providing data that will enable assigned personnel to make the proper revisions and modifications to the program.

The evaluation group will publish a yearly evaluation report and submit it to the principal and make copies available for the Superintendent of Schools.

Figure 4-2

The first part of this chapter has examined new program planning and evaluation techniques. A more generalized overview of program evaluation is now appropriate.

EVALUATING EXISTING PROGRAMS

For purposes of clarification, I will classify programs into two categories: the first consists of programs already in existence; the second, new programs that will be developed by the planning group once it is established. At this point I wish to reflect on the program that already is in operation and has not yet been evaluated for effectiveness.

Prior to evaluating any existing program, a school needs to clearly see each program in its present perspective. Having little or no base with which staff can carry on a dialogue for future evaluation is analogous to expecting a newborn infant to read. Thus, it is important to construct a brief but concise synopsis of each academic program.

Emphasis is placed on deriving input from representative staff, and the finished product should be a result of consensus, if not total agreement, of all subject area teachers.

The program description may be as voluminous and detailed as is felt to be necessary to be fully understood. Where possible, it is recommended that the program description be limited to one page. A program description should include the following:

1. Subject title
2. Major goals
3. Present program
4. Recent developments
5. Program needs

A sample program overview:

ENGLISH LANGUAGE PROGRAM OVERVIEW 9-12

MAJOR GOALS
The English language program hopes to provide students with:

Proficiency in understanding and using the English language.

Proficiency in writing, speaking and other communication skills.

The skills, techniques and attitudes necessary to make judgments.

Positive self-concept.

PRESENT PROGRAM

The K-12 program is designed to provide exposure to, experience with, and mastery of basic and advanced skills in the areas of reading, speaking, handwriting, spelling, composition, listening-viewing, doing, comprehending, reasoning, and applying language. Developmental in nature, the program is based on the concept of continuous progress through individualized learning and expanding degrees of English language skills.

At the high school level, the program (9-10), emphasizing the refinement of writing, reading, listening and speaking skills, is designed to prepare students for a two-year elective program (11-12) in the areas of literature, composition, and the communications-related areas of theater, speech, journalism, film and mass media. Students whose evaluated proficiency is low are directed into further developmental course work.

RECENT DEVELOPMENTS

A scope and sequence of developmental reading is being defined K-12. This scope identifies the major objectives of reading instruction and will have future implications for high school remedial offerings and basic competency skill expectations.

Sub-goals and objectives related to the four major English language program goals have been developed K-12.

Basic competency skill objectives are being developed to insure cohesive grade entry level skills. Additional phase two and three objectives are being developed to insure accelerated skill offerings and attempts are being made to accommodate gifted and talented students.

PROGRAM NEEDS

The continued development of reading and writing skill activities.

A. Establishment of a program of intensive exercise in sentence building and paragraphing.

Development of record keeping profile skill charts.

A continued updating of individualized instruction based upon proficiency evaluation.

Figure 4-3

No special evaluation problems exist where schools have established programs according to defined goals and measurable objectives. Where this is not the case or when goals and objectives are vague, inconsistent with school goals or not articulated with district programs, a redefinition activity is in order. Several questions need to be answered.

1. What was this program supposed to do?
2. Has it done what it was supposed to do?
3. How do we know what the program has done?
4. What priority does the program have now?
5. To update the quality of the program, does the program need
    A. Redefined goals and objectives
    B. Revisions
    C. Expansion
    D. Reduction
    E. Elimination
    F. Other (identify)

Evaluating existing programs and finding answers to the above questions may take several routes. This author believes that each school should have an evaluation team and each evaluation team must develop a school evaluation model designed to evaluate new and existing school programs. (See Chapters 5 and 6)

The absence of either or both of the above mentioned does not negate the possibility of doing some existing program evaluation. Initial program evaluation needs to both identify and evaluate existing programs so that they can be ranked in order of importance for future evaluation efforts. The following sample evaluation form both identifies and evaluates existing programs.

Existing Program Evaluation
Sheet #1
Initial Identification
and Evaluation

Directions: Please rate the following school programs Fair, Good, Very Good, Excellent or Eliminate. Where possible give supporting rationale. Use the back of this sheet if necessary.

Rating

1. Discipline review board program   ____
    Rationale:
2. Alternative elective program   ____
    Rationale:
3. Discretionary fund program   ____
    Rationale:
4. Volunteer program   ____
    Rationale:
5. High school tutorial program   ____
    Rationale:
6. HEART Special Reading Program   ____
    Rationale:
7. PROJECT SMART Math Program   ____
    Rationale:
8. Special Math Lab Program   ____
    Rationale:
9. Spelling Improvement Program   ____
    Rationale:
10. Other programs not listed
    A.   ____
    B.   ____
    C.   ____

Figure 4-4

Ratings will often turn up programs in need of further evaluation and they offer you, as principal, some clear indication of the priority which should be attached to each program. By substituting your own specific school programs, you will have a good sense of existing program status.

Developing a questionnaire will help to assess existing problems and/or evaluate success. Questionnaire feedback often provides insights into further evaluation needs and ways to approach them. The following sample questionnaire guide was designed for use in the Westport, Connecticut Schools and is offered here in partial context.

Questionnaire #1   Date _____

This guide is intended to facilitate the assessment of an instructional program. Information submitted in response to the points raised in the guide forms a substantive part of the data with which a committee will work as it prepares its analysis and recommendations for further planning and development. It is essential, therefore, that those responding be as explicit and informative as possible. Thank you for your responses.

A. *Personnel*
    1. Name _____ Position _____
    2. School(s) Assignment _____ Grade(s) _____
    3. Extra Assignments: (Co-curricular, supervisory, extra-curricular) _____

B. *Pupils*
    1. Number of students you work with daily (In classes) _____.
    2. Number of class periods you teach (daily or weekly: indicate which):
    _____
    3. Comments _____
    _____

C. *The Program*   *Yes*   *No*
    1. Do you have an established program for each   ____   ____
    grade?
    2. Is your program both coordinated and articulated?
    (Coordinated means relatively uniform in goals, objectives, materials and methods from school to school at a grade level.

Articulated means joined together in some logical way, grade
by grade, K-12)   *Yes*   *No*

       (a) Coordinated? ____ ____
       (b) Articulated?   ____ ____

3. If "no," do you feel that it is important that your program
be coordinated and articulated?   ____ ____
Please explain why or why not _____

_____

_____

_____

4. Is your program regarded as one which has a basic content,
the importance of which is paramount to parents and teachers
alike?   ____ ____

5. If "no," is your program area regarded as one in which the
basic skills of the area and the concepts of the area may be
served equally well through any of a number of contents?

                                                   ____ ____

6. Are the skills of your program area unique to your area,
not taught elsewhere and generally incapable of being sup-
ported by other areas?   ____ ____

7. If other areas share skills with your area, what are these
areas? Please list _____

_____

_____

D. *Specific Program Strengths*

    1. As you reflect on your program, please cite what you be-
lieve are the strengths of your program as revealed by hard
evidence. The following are a number of hard items you may
wish to consider: kind and quantity of texts, supplements,
supplies, visual aids, instructional equipment; the school
schedule, time allocations, colleague and support personnel;
pupil diagnosis and counselor support, identification of learning problems, provision of special or gifted pupils; pupil
achievement, pupils who distinguish themselves, perform-
ances rendered, projects completed, honors or awards or
achievements of special merit from school and nonschool
source.

_____
_____
_____
_____

2. Please comment on what you believe to be those factors which are most conducive to producing the strengths your programs possess?

_____
_____
_____

E. *Program Weaknesses*
   1. As you reflect on your program, please cite what you believe are the weaknesses of your program as revealed by hard evidence. The previously listed items may serve as suggestions here too.

_____
_____
_____
_____

2. Please comment on what you believe to be those factors which are most conducive to producing the weaknesses you identify.

_____
_____
_____

F. *Program Materials*   *Yes   No*
   1. Do you have sufficient materials to teach your program?

                                              ____   ____
   2. Are the materials up-to-date?   ____   ____
   3. Is there a supplementary materials supply available to you?

                                              ____   ____
   4. Please comment on the adequacy and recency of materials in your area.

_____
_____
_____

Figure 4-5

Other means of evaluating existing programs include gauging the reaction of parents, community, staff, students and other administrators to the program. Norm reference tests may give some indications that programs are succeeding or are experiencing difficulty. In using norm tests in evaluating existing programs, do not overreact to test results. Norm tests often provide a signal. The question is: How big is the signal given out and of what importance is it in program evaluation? Once the signal is evident, further examination is necessary.

1. What is the characteristic of the group's ability?
2. Does actual school performance relate to test performance?
3. What, if any, test deficiences are in evidence?
4. Does the program teach what the test measures?
5. If the program is changed, will there be any significant difference?
6. Are additional evaluation activities called for before change is considered?

Several means of evaluating existing programs are available for school use; however, emphasis should be placed on developing a school evaluation model designed to measure all programs in a consistent systematic manner.

THE ROLE OF EVALUATION IN PROGRAM DEVELOPMENT

Program planning begins with the establishment of program goals and objectives, and these should be evaluated as they are developed in terms of actual school needs, ability to provide resources, appropriateness to present programs and estimated results. A yardstick for measuring the potential validity of developed goals and objectives needs to be established by the school planning group. In this manner, inappropriate goals and objectives are discarded by means of a preliminary evaluation procedure.

Each stage of program development should build upon the previous stage and provisions must be made for revising, modifying and discarding based upon established evaluation procedures. Implementation plans need to include provisions for continual field-testing activities, designed to provide essential data needed for the decision-makers to make necessary program changes.

EXAMINING PROGRAM EVALUATION CONSTRAINTS

The complexity of any school operation denotes certain built-in program planning and evaluation constraints. The degree and type of constraints vary in proportion to the degree of uniqueness of each school within its own district and the district's uniqueness with relation to other districts. Each program will also have its own unique constraints that differentiate certain evaluation characteristics. Essentially, program evaluation constraints are identifying factors and variables that influence cause-effect relationships, and they should be seriously considered when evaluation results are analyzed. Program evaluation constraints often preclude that certain goals and objectives, or portions thereof, will be difficult or impossible to reach because of existing or forecast conditions. When constraints are of such a magnitude that they readily identify inability to bring about change, the program planning process should recommend curtailment of continued planning or a change in the existing program.

Program evaluation constraints are classified into two categories—general and specific. General constraints consist of district and school conditions and regulations which can be identified as having an effect on the success of the program in question. Specific program evaluation constraints revolve around program development implementation or existing program operation. Both general and specific constraints usually identify the fact that certain conditions will have to be overcome or compensated for and these need to be considered in the total program evaluation process.

The following program evaluation constraints have been taken from several schools as an example of general constraints:

1. The district has operated on a policy of no new programs if they call for additional paid personnel. Volunteer help

may be used and existing staff time may be reallocated where appropriate.

2. Our school was built to accommodate 900 students. Present enrollment stands at 1010 with future increases forecast. This factor taxes our existing facilities to the limit and seriously hinders program flexibility.

3. Budget allocations call for a five percent increase next year for our school. At this point five percent will hardly cover existing program costs. New programs considerations will have to make provisions for this condition.

4. Our school is presently on a waiver approval from the State Department of Education for violation of minimum standards. It is possible that some existing programs may have to be dropped to comply with state expectations.

5. Because of increased teaching loads, members of the program planning group and the evaluation team will experience difficulty in finding time to perform their duties.

6. Existing program goals and objectives are being criticized by the community and pressure is mounting to eliminate a number of programs that are not directly related to the back-to-the-basics movement.

Specific evaluation constraints are usually readily identifiable in any school program. Constraints for a Language Arts program could also be written like this:

1. Our inability to reconcile differing concepts as to what constitutes a Language Arts program.

2. Varying staff backgrounds and a lack of an inservice program for teachers of Language Arts.

3. Our inability to come up with ways to measure the success of all established Language Arts objectives.

4. A communication gap exists between what the community knows about our Language Arts program and what we think they know.

5. The lack of an agreed upon sequential-articulated grade level Language Arts program.

6. The lack of activity and experience centered areas within our building.

MAKING PROVISIONS FOR SEQUENTIAL STEP EVALUATIONS

Program planning is a continuous, ongoing process subject to constant recycling and revision. Evaluation must provide the data and rationale necessary for recycling and revision to be meaningful. For this reason several approaches to periodic evaluation should be explored by those responsible for evaluating school programs.

The two most common sequential evaluation patterns revolve around time allotments and program step implementation. To satisfy time evaluation criteria, a number of pre-determined evaluations are conducted at a prescribed time throughout the life of the program, usually x number of times during any given school year. In this manner, the date for initial evaluation is established and each subsequent evaluation date is recorded and adhered to. The following evaluation report represents a sample of the second of six evaluations conducted on the progress of a middle school individualized math program.

Hopeville Middle School

Department Evaluation Report

Program Hope Math

Evaluation #2 of 6

Date December 21

Major goal
progress:

With the exception of 18 students, all middle school students are involved with the Hope Math program at least 50% of the time. It appears that we may not be able to involve every student.

Major objectives
progress:

Much to our disappointment no significant change can be reported based on evaluation #2 data. While a substantial number of youngsters have reached prescribed objectives, it appears that an equal number suffered the summer "failure to retain" syndrome. They should be up-to-date by February.

Method of
evaluation: Pre-test administered in June before students left for summer vacation. Post-test evaluations have been given in October and December. Tests are Series E type. In addition teachers responded to observation questionnaire #2.

Previous methods
used if different
from above: No additional methods used at this time.

Recommendations
based on
evaluation data: Even though the evaluation data reveals that no significant difference has occurred to date, the department feels that students are at the turning point, and the program should continue.

Additional
evaluation
requests: The department feels that this evaluation would be more valid if it were possible to establish a control/non-control group setting for the balance of the year.

Figure 4-6

Program step implementation evaluations may follow a similar pattern as described above. Program developments determine the evaluation application rather than a previously prescribed time-frame. Each program revision or modification may in turn speed up or delay the next evaluation. The sequence remains important, but it is not tied to a specified time period. There are many approaches to sequential evaluation and each school should adapt or adopt those that are most appropriate for its own purposes. In this complex world of evaluation, the two approaches just discussed appear to this author to be the most practical and the easiest for school use.

HOW TO EVALUATE LONG-TERM PROGRAMS

Programs that are designed to have a long-term effect need to be evaluated continuously and for an extended period of time, usually from three to five years. Programs in this category might include dropout prevention, vandalism reduction, parent volunteers, gifted and talented, co-curricular, and other programs that by their structure can not be evaluated properly without long-term provisions.

Most programs similar to the above mentioned require two approaches to evaluation—one involves a continued monitoring evaluation of the program operation (long-term) to ascertain whether, in fact, the program is doing what it was intended to do. (Example: Are we successful in reducing the number of dropouts each year?)

An evaluation questionnaire, designed to evaluate how well a specific academic program at Hartford High School in White River Jct., Vt., prepares a student to handle college academic work appears below.

Follow up evaluation from Hartford High School graduates

#6 Writing Skills Preparation

College Students

Graduates of 1976—1979

The staff and administration of Hartford High School are interested in obtaining information from Hartford High School graduates. This information will be helpful in providing guidelines for determining long-range goals and objectives for the education of future students at Hartford High School and the Vocational Center.

Your cooperation is appreciated.

To be answered by all graduates who entered college.

1. Year of graduation _____
2. Number of writing courses taken _____
3. Did other English courses emphasize writing skills?   Yes __ No __
   If yes, which ones. _____ _____
4. Did English writing courses stress:
   A. Creativity of expression _____
   B. Grammatical achievement _____
   C. Both of the above _____
5. Did other subject areas demand written standards similar to ones employed by the English department?   Yes __ No __
   A. If yes, which ones. _____ _____
6. Do you feel there were enough writing courses available to you?   _____
   _____
   A. If yes, did you take what you needed? _____
   B. Would you advise future college bound students to take more writing in high school? _____
7. Did you experience difficulty with college level writing requirements? _____
   A. If yes, what would you attribute your difficulty to?
   _____
   _____
   _____
8. What improvements in the English writing program do you feel would best serve future college students? _____
   _____
   _____

Please use the back of this form to comment on any of these questions.

Please return this survey to:

Follow-Up Evaluation Study

Hartford High School

White River Jct., Vt. 05001

Figure 4-7

A similar approach is used by Hampton High School in Hampton, Nebraska, to evaluate the overall instructional program. Student background questions have been removed to more adequately display evaluation questions.

Hampton High School

Hampton Public School District

Hampton, Nebraska

1. Your name _____

2. Year in which you graduated from Hampton High School

   _____

3. What were your educational or vocational plans when you graduated from high school? _____

   _____

   _____

4. The following questions ask your opinion about the program of studies and the quality of the instruction you received in high school. Please be frank and honest in your response.

   (a) Were the courses which you took in high school helpful to you in your present position? Explain briefly.

   _____

   _____

   (b) List the three subjects which have proven to be of greatest value to you since graduation.

   1. _____ 3. _____

   2. _____

(c) List the three subjects which have proven to be of least value to you since graduation.

1. _____
2. _____
3. _____

(d) What subjects do you feel should have been offered which were not available?

1. _____
2. _____
3. _____

(e) What was your reaction to the quality of the instruction in the classes which you took during high school? _____

_____

_____

(f) Were there high school activities (outside the regular classroom) which you wanted to participate in but were not able to do so? What changes in this part of the school program would you recommend? _____

_____

_____

5. What would you list as the three strongest aspects of your high school experience in Hampton High School?

1. _____
2. _____
3. _____

6. What would you list as the three most significant limitations or weaknesses of your experience in Hampton High School?

1. _____
2. _____
3. _____

7. What three things would you like to see be done which would, in your judgement, improve the high school experience for future graduates of Hampton High School?

1. _____
2. _____
3. _____

8. Please make any additional comments which you feel
    are relevant.

Figure 4-8

Another long-term evaluation approach utilizes the control
group—experimental group method of data collection. The control group continues to function in the regular existing program
while the experimental group takes part in new program implementation. A typical control/non control evaluation will offer
some sort of pre-test upon entering the program, a test at the end
of the first year, second year and the third year if desired. At the
end of the first year, a new group is selected to start, and the procedure is followed with a new group the beginning of the third
year. All three groups are followed and data collected until the
third group completes the cycle. At that point evaluation data is
compared, analyzed and decisions are made. Another long term
evaluation your school might wish to use is the year-to-year internal and external comparative data approach. (External: with
other schools in the district)

SUMMARY

The school program planning group provides a mechanism
for developing and evaluating the program planning process.
Where possible, separate planning and evaluation groups should
be established. The program planning and evaluation format falls
into two categories: existing programs and proposed new programs. The most important prerequisite to sound program planning evaluation is the development of program descriptions.
Without adequate program descriptions, meaningful evaluation
is, at best, left to chance.

Because the complexities of school operations denote built-in
program planning and evaluation constraints, they need to be
seriously considered when analyzing evaluation results and during the decision making process.

Other major factors to consider for a complete program
planning and evaluation program include the development of sequential step evaluations and evaluation of long-term programs.

Establishing the School 5

Evaluation Team

School evaluation becomes more widely accepted by staff when it is planned and implemented internally. Evaluation carried out by school personnel tends to be less threatening to teachers when it is developed and led by a group of peers and other representative people. The school evaluation team approach offers an effective evaluation mechanism.

ENSURING PARITY WITH STAFF REPRESENTATION

As principal, you have the responsibility for determing what the composition of the evaluation team should be. A major guideline should be to make sure that the team is as representative of the school as possible. Parity is an important consideration and where practical students, teachers, parents and administrators should be represented as participating members of the team.

Since student growth plays such a large role in evaluation of the effectiveness of any school, *students* should be included on the team in some manner. Students often provide valuable insights as school program receivers. The size of the team will be a limiting factor on the number of students who may participate. Students selected should be in a position to communicate with the rest of the student body. A class officer, student council representative or other school governing body member will usually fill the bill.

Parents are entitled to a voice in what a school should do and how it should do it. Therefore, no school evaluation team is complete without at least one parent representative. *Teachers* have the most pronounced influence on how effective a school is and they should have the largest representation on the evaluation team. You, as *principal,* or your designee should complete the membership of the team.

A SAMPLE EVALUATION TEAM DESCRIPTION

The importance of developing a descriptive display for the school evaluation team cannot be overemphasized. It is important for team members to be thoroughly aware of the operational intent of their team, and it is equally important that all other parties be able to understand what the evaluation team is expected to do and how.

The evaluation team's operational description should be brief but concise. The old adage, "If it can't be explained on one sheet of paper, it's too long," may be appropriate. You may need to develop your own descriptive criteria in addition to the following:

1. Team goal
2. Major objective
3. Status
4. Training
5. Budgetary considerations

6. Membership
7. Meeting schedule
8. Reporting procedure
9. Miscellaneous

Filled in, the sample evaluation operational team description might look like this:

Evaluation Group

(Operational Description)

Goal:

To identify and develop a consistent mode of operation that will be utilized for all evaluation procedures in the school.

Major
Objective:

The evaluation group will, by June of 1980, design a working model for evaluation in the following areas:
1. Staff evaluation
2. School programs
3. Academic progress

Status:

The evaluation group shall have ongoing responsibility for determining the effectiveness of all programs designed and implemented in this school.

Training:

Members of the evaluation group shall develop expertise in evaluation techniques through attendance at conferences, workshops, visitations and the purchase of written materials.

Budgetary
Considerations:

The evaluation group chairman will develop, with the principal, a display of resources needed to accomplish identified goals and objectives.

Membership: High school assistant principal, chair-
                    person
                    Social studies teacher
                    Math teacher
                    English teacher
                    Science teacher
                    Guidance counselor
                    One student
                    One parent

Meeting
Schedule: The evaluation group shall meet on the
                    second and fourth Wednesdays of the
                    month and at other times deemed
                    necessary by the chairperson.

Reporting
Procedure: The evaluation group will report di-
                    rectly to the principal monthly and on
                    other occasions as deemed necessary
                    by the group or the principal.

Miscellaneous: The chairperson shall make released
                    time and remuneration arrangements
                    whenever necessary.

Figure 5-1

THE PRINCIPAL'S ROLE ON THE EVALUATION TEAM

After the team has been established, you are obligated to continue as an active participating member as the team attempts to
develop and implement an effective evaluation program. Where
administrative duties are such that you must designate this responsibility, you should endeavor to lend support to the group
throughout its continued existence.

As principal, you have several roles to play as a member of
the evaluation team:

1. Leader   The instructional leader of the school must
                       also become leader of the evaluation

	team. If that leadership role is designated to another, the designee should have enough expertise to handle the role effectively.
2. Instructor	We have previously established that the principal needs to develop essential evaluation skills to oversee the total evaluation program. In his role on the evaluation team, the principal must instruct other members so that they may acquire equal skills.
3. Catalyst	Coinciding with his resource role, the principal must be able to insert ideas, suggestions, questions and other information necessary to keep the team going when it begins to reach a plateau. At times, he may have to make operational decisions for the team.
4. Interpreter	The principal must be able to interpret the evaluation team's work to teachers, students, parents, central office staff, school board and the community at large.
5. Communicator	Program publicity should fall within the scope of the principal's role. It is important to have the team's efforts publicized through flyers, school newsletters, and the local media.
6. Liaison	Consistent with the role of interpreter and communicator, the principal needs to serve as the go-between for all parties involved. Special emphasis should be placed on those outside of the school, i.e., parents and other community members.

Not mentioned, but certainly implied, is the principal's role as number one BOOSTER! No school evaluation program will reach its potential without the principal cheering it on.

SETTING UP THE TEAM RESOURCE LIBRARY

Once in operation, each team member will have varying degrees of evaluation expertise. For most members it will be a learning experience, one in which evaluation skills will have to be acquired. Workshops, conferences, resource persons and visitations will help most members acquire some insights and skills but will not be sufficient for all needs. It is important that you help the evaluation team set up its own evaluation resource library. Library materials should be made available to other staff members when not in use by the evaluation team.

Where do we find the resource material? Two members of the team should be responsible for compiling a bibliography of available books, pamphlets, monographs, filmstrips, etc., that cover the broad spectrum of evaluation. Several excellent listings of educational resource materials can be acquired from the following sources:

> Administrative Resources Division
> Capitol Publications, Inc.
> 2430 Pennsylvania Avenue, N.W.
> Washington, D.C. 20037
> Publication: *Books for Today's Educator,* published periodically throughout the year

> Educational Research Service, Inc.
> 1815 North Fort Meyer Drive
> Arlington, Virginia 22209
> Publication: *ERS Annotated Bibliography: The Evaluation of Instructional Programs*

> Parker Publishing Co., Inc.
> West Nyack, New York 10994
> Publication: *Book News Brochure; Education: Elementary-Secondary*

Additional resources are located in the bibliography section of this book.

Where should the resource library be located? Resource materials should be readily available for evaluation team members' use. Possible resource locations include, in priority:

1. Unused room	Advantages include privacy and opportunities to openly discuss evaluation team progress and problems. Combined meeting room and resource room is desirable.
2. Reserved section in the library	Advantages include central location and easy access. Possible inability to carry on open discussions without disrupting library operations have to be considered.
3. Teachers' room	Ready access and availability are positive points. Other teacher activities tend to impede team work.
4. Principal's office	Least desirable of all locations but acceptable if others are not available. Accessibility most often presents a problem. The principal is often tied up behind closed doors when other members want to use resources.

PREPARING FOR THE FIRST MEETING

Setting the stage for the first evaluation team meeting is an important consideration for you, as principal. Having well-informed people ready to begin the first meeting without undue orientation work can increase the enthusiasm of members and enhance the progress of the team. To prepare members for the first meeting you should:

1. Prepare agenda items in advance.

2. Send a short note welcoming members to the team.

3. Announce the time and place of the meeting.

4. Enclose the team operational description.

5. Describe the agenda—allow for flexibility.

6. Plan to keep the first meeting relatively short.

7. Plan the meeting so input from each member is insured.

8. Encourage members to discuss agenda items with you beforehand.

9. List any instructions necessary for membership preparation.

The following is an example of a memo sent out to an evaluation group in preparation for its first meeting.

To: M. McAvoy, E. Allen, J. Meagher, M. Mock, R. Thomas, P. Bouthillier, D. Manchester—otherwise known as the Evaluation Team.

From: F. E. Kenison, Principal

Welcome! Now that the membership of this group has been identified, it is imperative we have a meeting soon. Our target date:

>Wednesday, November 17, 9:00 a.m.
>Guidance Conference Room
>Hartford High School

Enclosed is a copy of the "Team Operational Description." You may wish to raise some questions before our meeting regarding the contents of the operational description. I cannot promise all the answers but should be able to respond to most questions.

Our first agenda should be concerned with:

>An overview of evaluation as it relates to a management system
>Organizaton
>Task description
>Identification of resources
>Setting a meeting format—dates, place, length of meetings, etc.

We will allow time for these agenda areas to be expanded if need be, and each member will be asked for ideas, suggestions and/or recommendations for follow-up activities.

If you need a substitute to cover your regular assignment, see your department head or immediate supervisor to make proper arrangements. He/She may verify the need by seeing me, or this memo should be sufficient. Please bring your reference materials with you.

Our first meeting will not go beyond 12 noon.

Figure 5-2

Conducting the first meeting according to the organizational plan is an important must. Before the first meeting is over you and the evaluation team should be ready to discuss a number of other team operations such as resources, roles, goals and other team considerations.

ALLOCATING RESOURCES TO THE EVALUATION TEAM

To function effectively and reach stated goals and objectives, the evaluation team will need to have certain resources available. Resources might include some or all of the following areas: Budget, Staff, Clerical, Inservice, Materials and Time. Each school evaluation team will have different resource needs and varying degrees of built-in resource availability. The lack of protected resources should not be a hindrance to establishing an evaluation team. Careful reorganization of in-school resources will permit any school to move ahead with this valuable addition to its total operation.

Resource needs should be determined once the goals and objectives of the team have been established. A wish-list outlining desirable resources should be developed by the team. From this list, you will have to determine how much is or can be made available and what alternatives you and the team can develop to compensate for resources not available.

Following the above guidelines, an evaluation team resource list would look similar to Figure 5-3.

DEFINING TEAM MEMBER ROLES

Each member of the school evaluation team should have his role defined. Where possible, separate role descriptions may be developed for each evaluation sub-group role established, i.e., program, staff, testing-measurement and other committee assignments. Assignments should be recorded and entered into the minutes and reviewed periodically by the evaluation team.

Where total school programs are to be evaluated, it is best to include more than one parent and student on the team. When a

(Checklist and Cost Sheet)

b1

Resources Identified	Cost	Source	Available Yes	No	Alternative
1. Two conferences					
A. N.A.S.E.	$ 500.00	Inservice account	X		Consultant
B. McGraw-Hill (3 members)	75.00			X	
2. Visitation Fopp School (All members) Systren, Tenn.	$ 100 for substitutes es $ 15 for travel	District Substitute Fund	? X		Visit on in-service day
3. Compensation for members	$ 1200	District Funds		X	Released time
4. Reference Library	$ 100?	Code 25001 Other expenses	X		
5. Consultant	$ 100	Program development	?		State Dept. Personnel
6. Equipment and other materials	?	Existing school inventory	X		
7. Misc. supplies	$ 30	Code 25001 Other expenses and existing school inventory	X		
8. Refreshments (coffee, etc.)	$ 25	School activity account	X		

Figure 5-3

specific program or sub-program is to be evaluated, the need for more than one parent and/or student member decreases.

Team member roles may be divided into three categories: general roles, specific roles and other role definitions. General roles for all members may include the following:

1. Serve as school-program evaluators
2. Serve as resource personnel for school faculty
3. Conduct evaluation inservice workshops
4. Function as an advisory group for the decision makers
5. Make program recommendations based on evaluation data

Specific roles should be developed and written for:

1. Chairman
2. Recorder
3. Sub-committees
4. District representative
5. Faculty liaison
6. Publicity

Other role definitions should be established for each of the following:

1. Parent   4. Central office (ex officio)
2. Student   5. Outside consultant
3. Teacher   6. Others?

SETTING GOAL PARAMETERS FOR THE TEAM

No evaluation team can operate successfully without having rather clearly defined goal parameters. Goal parameters should delineate the scope of the team's operation! Should it be responsible for evaluating every aspect of the school operation, or should it focus on more concrete areas? Since the concept of the evaluation team will be foreign to most members and other faculty, it is best to start slowly and add on in ensuing years. The first year may be devoted to one important area such as program evaluation or expanded to include staff evaluation if the team is large enough to break into two sub-groups.

Goals and sub-goals need to be identified and appropriate objectives listed.

Hopeville School

(Evaluation Team Goals)

Sample

Major Goal:	To provide the school with two working evaluation models that will enable the school to measure its effectiveness in the areas of program and staff evaluation.
Sub-goal:	To develop an evaluation program which will encourage and afford all school personnel the opportunity to participate in the evaluation process.
Objectives:	The evaluation program will be ongoing with a major emphasis on providing data that will enable assigned personnel to make the proper revisions and modifications to instructional programs.
	The evaluation team will monitor two specific instructional programs and one staff evaluation program for the school year ensuing. Monitoring reports will be issued every six weeks.
	The evaluation team will offer a series of five workshops on the school evaluation model. Workshops will begin in January and end in May.

> Where practical, the evaluation team will offer alternative solutions to program problems. The solutions are to be weighed by the staff and principal.
>
> The evaluation group will publish a yearly evalaution report and submit same to the principal and staff.

Figure 5-4

To accomplish Figure 5-4 objectives, the team needs to establish who is asking the questions and who wants to know the results. When results, alternatives and/or recommendations are given, it is important to ascertain who is going to make decisions.

ESTABLISHING COMMUNICATIONS GUIDELINES FOR THE TEAM

Communication must be a major concern of the evaluation team. Guidelines need to be established for communicating with each other, the principal, staff and other decision makers. The nature of the team assignment dictates close and continual contact and a sharing of ideas among members. This may be accomplished by designating time blocks two to three times a week to meet informally to discuss problems, suggestions, progress, etc. Secondly, the team will establish its communication mode through its formally scheduled meetings. Input from all members is essential, and it is the responsibility of the chairman to see that communication flows freely between members. The minutes of each meeting should officially serve as the team's communication mechanism for members, faculty, principal and designated central office staff.

You should establish with the team, procedures for communicating with you if you do not serve as a member of the team. You may elect to do this by having your designee report directly to you. Arrangements may be made to visit the team meetings occasionally to be updated on team progress.

Regardless of the approaches used to insure sound communication procedures, they should not be left to chance. Communications may seem like a small concern within the scope of the total evaluation task, but properly planned, it makes for harmonious relations and improves the effectiveness of the team operation.

EVALUATING TEAM PROGRESS

Any new school program should have provisions for ongoing evaluation and recycling when necessary. The same conditions and guidelines should apply to the school evaluation team. The team operational description will provide a base to measure goal and objective achievement as well as other operational procedures. The team should establish its own evaluation methods and a time-frame for evaluating progress.

An evaluation checklist may prove useful to a team trying to determine what it has accomplished.

Evaluation Team

(Evaluation checklist)

Partial Sample

                                                           Yes   No

1. Goals and objectives have been established by the team.
2. The purpose and major goal of the team has been communicated to the rest of the faculty.
3. All team organization details have been established and agreed to.
4. Roles and assignments have been clearly defined.
5. Methods of communications have been established.
6. Progress reporting procedures are operational.
7. Established time-frames for model development are on target.

Yes No

8. Provisions for recycling changes have been
   made.

Figure 5-5

The evaluation team is a relatively new concept that offers immeasurable opportunities for people to become more involved in measuring the effectiveness of their own schools. Its most positive feature is that it is internal and everyone can be a part of the evaluation process. It also has the advantage of immediate and constant feedback which offers a sound basis for constructive change.

SUMMARY

The school evaluation team offers an effective evaluation mechanism and should be highly successful if care is taken to insure that the team is as representative of the school as possible. Your role as an active participant in the team operation cannot be over-emphasized.

Other important ingredients of an effective team operation include:

1. Establishment of a team resource library.
2. Proper preparation for the first meeting.
3. Allocation of sufficient resources to the team.
4. Team member role definitions.
5. Goal parameters for the team.
6. Communication guidelines for the team.
7. Team progress evaluation.

Designing 6

The Evaluation Model

Most evaluation models that have appeared to date have been developed by evaluation theorists. Because opinions differ on what constitutes a good model, no attempt will be made to recommend a particular model. This chapter will focus on the evaluation model as a practical and efficient way for local schools to evaluate their own effectiveness.

DETERMINING PRIORITIES FOR EVALUATION

The more advanced the development of school goals and objectives, the greater the chance for carrying out successful evaluations. Sloppy goal and objective organization almost always denotes a sloppy evaluation. It is important that any evaluation
model developed be consistent with previously developed school
program goals and objectives. School goals and objectives will help
to identify priority areas in need of evaluation, but provisions
should be made to find hidden areas that might escape the normal
selection process.

Often priorities will be determined by either external or
internal concerns and/or demands of teachers, parents and certain special interest pressure groups. Under these conditions,
priorities for evaluation are often dictated rather than selected.
Because priority evaluation needs emerge from a variety of
sources, each school district and individual school should develop
evaluation models to meet any evaluation need.

FITTING THE MODEL TO THE SCHOOL ENVIRONMENT

The number and various types of evaluation models available
continue to grow as the need and demand for greater accountability increases. The easiest approach to designing an evaluation
model for a school is to pick from those available and simply adopt
one. After all, why reinvent the wheel and spend long hours developing a model for our school? This approach may work in
some cases, but chances are the staff will be less likely to understand or readily accept a model that they have not helped to design. For this reason, evaluation models should be designed to
coincide with district models and also to take into consideration
the unique characteristics of the school.

School evaluation models fall basically into three categories:
program, staff and total school operation. Program models should
be flexible enough to evaluate both regular school programs
(math, reading, French, etc.) and other more specialized pro-

grams, i.e., independent study, activity, elective and dropout prevention. Schools with more specialized and diversified programs need to consider a more comprehensive model that will accommodate, with few exceptions, all program evaluations.

DESIGNING THE SCHOOL EVALUATION MODEL

The initial task of the school evaluation committee should be to design an evaluation model, based upon an established goal, that will cover school operations. The goal may be to provide a model that will be simple enough to offer all professionals the opportunity to participate in the evaluation process, or it may be designed to meet imposed requirements for accountability. Each school will have its own basic evaluation needs that will help determine the goal selected.

The evaluation model should:

1. Allow the school evaluation committee to examine any program selected.
2. Develop evaluation criteria and procedures before program implementation.
3. Provide for ongoing evaluation to take care of program "fixits" along the way.
4. Develop specific criteria for each program sub-area identified.
5. Provide sufficient evaluation data for the decision-makers to make intelligent decisions.
6. Help determine whether change is economically feasible or whether it will make any difference.
7. Make provisions, where applicable, for large scale parent, student, teacher and administrator involvement.
8. Take into consideration personnel expertise and other resource limitations.
9. Be flexible enough to be easily revised or modified.
10. Be simple enough for everyone to understand and use.

HOW TO SIMPLIFY THE EVALUATION PROCESS

The reference in the above list to a model that is simple enough for everyone to understand and use has a special significance. This author firmly believes that the lack of evaluation expertise in schools today is a result of two factors. First, teacher training institutions fail to provide sufficient training at the undergraduate and graduate levels, and second, where courses are offered, they are so filled with evaluation jargon and technical operations that they are of little or no use to the average school practitioner. Also, most local inservice and/or staff development programs are ill-equipped to handle school evaluation needs.

The professional evaluator often argues that too much of what is or passes for school evaluation today is dangerously oversimplified. The educational practitioner will argue that evaluation is so complex that it is too difficult to comprehend and, consequently, impractical for the typical school operation.

When professional educators do not understand and are unable to work effectively with the evaluation program, they will find a way to avoid it. The evaluation model holds the key to simplifying the evaluation process; it should be brief but concise, impressive but practical and easily put into operation. There are no magical formulas to simplify the process of evaluation; each school must work out its own formula that will:

- set the stage.
- proceed smoothly.
- provide data.
- offer viable alternatives.

The next section of this chapter will offer several examples of evaluation models designed to meet local needs.

EXAMPLES OF EVALUATION MODELS

The first evaluation model displayed is from the Birmingham Public Schools, Birmingham, Michigan. The *Birmingham Program*

Evaluation plan was prepared by a district evaluation committee, and it provides for district and building level evaluation. The building level section has been abstracted and is shown in Figure 6-1.

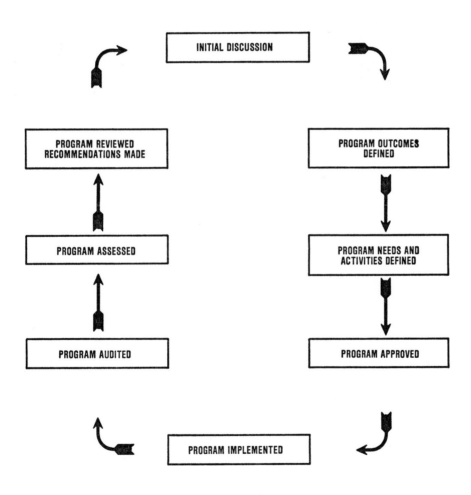

Figure 6-1

PROCEDURAL STEPS IN PROGRAM EVALUATION

I. **Step One: Program Nomination**
   B. *Building Level*
      1. Staff or citizens of the attendance area served by a school nominate programs to be evaluated through their *local* principal. Nominations must be in written form, addressed to the building principal, contain a brief rationale, and include a list of agencies or groups in support of the nomination.
      2. The building principal will send one copy of all requests to the Director of Curriculum or Deputy Superintendent for Administrative Services and one copy to the Chairman of the Evaluation Committee.
      3. The school principal will determine if the nominated program is to be evaluated. If it is, the principal will nominate a chairman of a Program Evaluation Advisory Committee (PEAC)* who will act as primary sponsor for the program evaluation.

II. **Step Two: Initial Discussions**
   B. *Building Level*
      1. The program sponsor meets with the principal, the Director of Evaluation, and any other individuals the principal designates to informally discuss program evaluation need and feasibility. Included in the discussion will be items pertaining to:
         a. Purpose of the evaluation
         b. Questions, Concerns to be addressed
         c. Evaluation procedures
         d. Estimated budget
         e. Timeline
         f. Audience for the report

III. **Step Three: Program Evaluation Plan Preparation**
   B. *Building Level*
      The PEAC, with assistance from the Department of Evaluation, prepares a program description that includes, as a minimum, the following information:

    1. An abstract of
      a. What the program is intended to accomplish
      b. When the program began
      c. When and how program progress has been reported to date
      d. The total fiscal support of the program
    2. A definition of evaluation plans that includes
      a. Purpose of the evaluation
      b. Questions, Concerns to be addressed
      c. Evaluation procedures
      d. Estimated budget
      e. Timeline
      f. Audience for the report

*Program Evaluation Advisory Committee may consist of:

Program sponsor	Other staff representation
Program staff representation	Parent representation
	Student representation

IV. Step Four: Program Evaluation Plan Review

  B. *Building Level*
    1. Plan submitted to Evaluation Committee for policy compliance check.
    2. Plan sent from Evaluation Committee to the appropriate school principal for review.
    3. Approved plan returned by the principal to the appropriate PEAC chairman.
    4. Principal forwards a copy of the approved plan to the appropriate division.

V. Step Five: Program Evaluation Activities Begun

District or building level program evaluation activities begun as proposed. Overall responsibility rests with the Department of Development and Evaluation.

VI. Step Six: Compile and Analyze Data; Prepare Technical Report

Technical report written by the Department of Evaluation with cooperation of PEAC members.

VII. **Step Seven: Technical Report Reviewed; Evaluation Report Written**

Appropriate PEAC's review technical report with the assistance of the Department of Development and Evaluation. Final evaluation report written by the Department of Evaluation.

VIII. **Step Eight: Final Evaluation Report Discussed**

Appropriate PEAC discuss report first with project participants, then with other interested parties.

IX. **Step Nine: Program Recommendations Made**

Final evaluation report submitted to appropriate division or principal.

X. **Step Ten: Program Directive Issued**

Decision made and directive issued by the appropriate deputy or principal.

Figure 6-2

The Birmingham plan provides a standard evaluation procedure for all program development. This type of evaluation model increases the credibility of any evaluation conducted.

Evaluation models need to include a descriptive overview of each component operation. The overview presented below is one example.

HARTFORD SCHOOL EVALUATION MODEL (Figure 6-3)

(Overview)

School Evaluation Committee — All evaluations conducted at the local building level will be channeled through the committee. Total district evaluation will be the responsibility of the district committee, and local school committees will assist when needed. The local committee will handle all evaluation requests and will make judgements on which programs should be evaluated.

	The committee may, at its discretion, initiate its own program evaluation at any time.
Program Identification	All new programs developed at the local school level are automatically identified for the evaluation process. Other programs, identified for evaluation, may result from needs assessment data, staff requests and administrator or school board requests.
Program Implementation Plan	The program evaluation plan must include the following components: 1. An outline of evaluation procedures including a sequential time-frame. 2. A list of evaluation resources needed to carry out the plan. 3. Method(s) to be used in reporting evaluation data. 4. Provisions for continued program recycling based on evaluation results.
Implementation Monitoring	Provisions for monitoring individual program component effectiveness should be expanded from the original evaluation plan. Constant monitoring of program development will provide the necessary evaluation data for making program changes.
Periodic Time Frame Evaluation	Designed to reinforce implementation monitoring procedures, periodic time-frame evaluation helps to validate the need for program change revisions. As a general guideline, no fewer than four and no more than eight time-frame evaluations should be conducted.
Recycling Program Operation	Data from implementation monitoring and periodic time-frame evaluations should be analyzed to make appropriate

HARTFORD SCHOOL EVALUATION MODEL
Hartford School District — White River Jct., Vt.

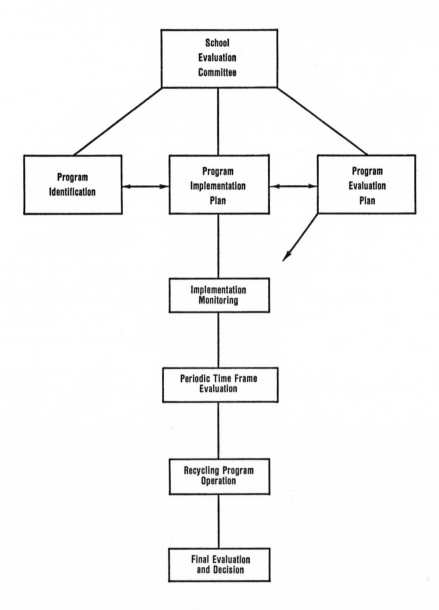

Figure 6-3

EVALUATION MODEL
Instructional Based Objective Programs

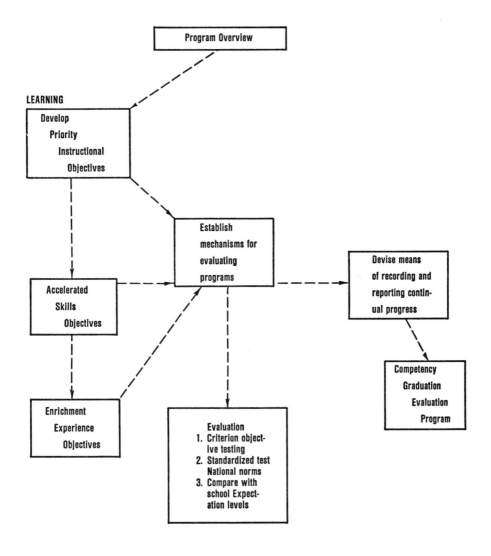

Figure 6-4

	program revisions. No changes should be made unless evaluation data shows that change is possible and that it will bring about program improvement. Proposed changes also must be economically feasible.
Final Evaluation and Decision	At some point in the life of any program, a final evaluation must be made and the future of the program spelled out. Initial final evaluation and decision dates may be changed only if ongoing evaluation shows that an extension would be in the best interest of the program. Approval for such an extension must come from the chairman of the evaluation committee and the administrator designated as the decision-maker.

Evaluation models may be designed for unique broad-based programs or for programs that may not be readily adapted to general school evaluation models. Figure 6-4 depicts a broad-based instructional program evaluation model.

Curriculum is another broad-based area that may require a separate evaluation model in your school. Figure 6-5 offers a sample curriculum evaluation model.

CURRICULUM STUDY EVALUATION
(Model)

Criteria	*Additional Information*
Define area to be studied	
1. Social studies elective grade eleven	"Political elections"
Background data	
1. Established two years ago	
2. Specific course goal	2. See page 2, course overview
3. Course objectives include	3. See page 3, course objectives
Components to be evaluated	
1. Course content	

2. Course objectives
3. Student participation
4. Student skill attainment

Evaluation time line

1. Past course operations by April 3	1. Obtain data from past two years
2. Present course offering Dec. 2, Feb. 27, April 3 and June 10	

Change status

1. Is change practical?	1. Last year's survey indicated several changes would bring about improvements.
2. Will evaluation make desired changes evident?	

Personnel Involvement

1. Course associates-personal evaluations	1. Teachers and department head
2. Evaluators	2. School evaluation team
3. Decision-makers	3. Curriculum coordinating committee and principal

Method of Evaluation

1. Questionnaire	1. Teachers, students, parents and administrators
2. Test scores	2. Quarterly
3. Observation	3. Teachers and department head
4. Objective analysis	4. Vote on objective success by teachers, department head and principal

Reporting Procedure

1. Written report	1. By school evaluation team
2. Conference with decision-maker	2. Recommendations requested

Figure 6-5

Special school programs sometimes are better evaluated by a specific evaluation model designed especially for the program. Often the regular school evaluation model or broad-based program model is too general and not equipped to handle the uniqueness of the program developed. Such a specific model is shown in Figure 6-6.

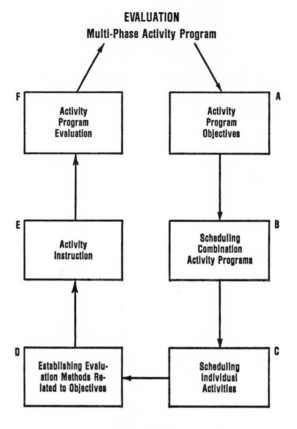

Figure 6-6

EVALUATING THE WHOLE CO-CURRICULAR
ACTIVITY PROGRAM

The evaluation model allows the evaluation committee to examine the total multi-phase program. In the evaluation model (Figure 6-6), we find a viable operational approach to evaluation. Evaluation begins with the establishment of activity program objectives and continues with scheduling procedures that insure maximum efficiency of operation. Careful consideration must be given to scheduling each program and individual activity within that program. If the multi-phase co-curricular activity program is to achieve success, it must be the first program plotted on the master schedule.

The evaluation model provides for evaluation criteria to be established before actual activity program instruction takes place. By building activity evaluation procedures into the ongoing operation, evaluation can be conducted on a continual basis and activity program changes made periodically, based upon derived evaluation results. It follows then that activity program objectives must be definitive enough to initially allow for measurable evaluation to take place periodically so that activities can be analyzed and improved.

Each activity should have objectives established before activity experiences take place. As the evaluation model indicates, the methods by which each activity will be evaluated have to be developed before the activity swings into operation. Evaluation methods may consist of teacher observations, parent questionnaires, teacher questionnaires, self-evaluations, and any number of other approaches.

The evaluation model must develop specific criteria for each major area. Activity program objectives must be consistent with school philosophy. Scheduling combination programs and individual activities should accomplish certain goals. Evaluation methods must reflect practical approaches to measuring success, and activity instruction should follow predetermined guidelines. Activity program evaluation criteria should make provisions for examination of the whole scope and sequence of the operation. Multi-phase operational guidelines appear underneath each model component.[2]

The C.I.P.P. Model

This author would be remiss if he did not mention the C.I.P.P. Evaluation Model developed originally by Daniel Stufflebeam and Egon Guba. Stufflebeam has been largely re-

---

[2]John Frank, Jr. *Complete Guide to Co-curricular Programs and Activities for the Middle Grades* (West Nyack, N.Y.: Parker Publishing Co., Inc., 1976), pp. 230–31.

sponsible for revising and modifying the model in recent years. Every administrator should familiarize himself with the advantages of the C.I.P.P. Model and explore its potential for school use. No attempt will be made to expand on its virtues in this book, but the reader will be referred to the C.I.P.P. Model and Stufflebeam's writings in the bibliography.

THE EVALUATION MATRIX

The evaluation matrix helps the evaluator and decision-maker to determine what specific segments of the program need improvement and in what priority. The evaluation decision-maker will find it helpful to fill in the evaluation matrix as evaluation progresses and results are made known. All evaluation participants should be recorded, including any outside evaluators. The evaluation matrix appears in Figure 6-7. The evaluation matrix should be followed up with a master evaluation progress chart, Figure 6-8 which will enable the principal to plot continual evaluation and revision progress.

GAINING APPROVAL OF THE SCHOOL EVALUATION MODEL

The evaluation model should offer a consistent and effective way to evaluate school programs. If it is to be used as a basic tool for accountability, it is a good idea to receive approval from the central office or at least review the model with appropriate central office staff. Provisions should be made to show that the model itself will be evaluated and its effectiveness determined at some point.

SUMMARY

The school evaluation model needs to be consistent with established school goals and objectives. School evaluation models should:

1. Allow the school evaluation committee to examine any program selected.

EVALUATION MATRIX
(SAMPLE)[3]

Rating 1-5:5 high

Activity		Student	Teacher	Administrator	Parent Advisors	Outside Evaluator
Brain Teasers	Average Rating	2	2	1	1	2
	Comments	Boring. Not enough materials	Lack of student interest. Difficulty finding new teasers.	Poor sign up. Poor attendance. Rapidly going downhill.		
Tournament Cribbage	Average Rating					
	Comments					
Movie Happenings	Average Rating					
	Comments					
Video Explorations	Average Rating					
	Comments					

Figure 6-7

MASTER EVALUATION PROGRESS CHART
(PARTIAL EXAMPLE)[4]

Rating 1-5:5 high

Activity	Activity Rating Number	Comment Rating	Recognized Needs	Proposed Remedy	Revision Results
Energy Crisis	3	Average	More practical experiences; Field trips	Get students into hands-on projects. Field trips to community problem areas. Enlist aid of electric co., stores, etc.	Improved to a 5 rating after one month
Baby-sitting	1	Poor overall	Not enough student interest and participation.	Drop this activity. Replace it with new activity from interest survey.	New activity started second marking period: Printmaking
Photo-graphy	5	Excellent—highly enjoyable and popular	Very few	Expand if possible.	
Electronics	4.5	Very popular—one of the best activities	More materials	More money for materials	Budget more next year or take money from activity fund.
Game Room	4	Popular activity; Enjoyable—fun	Only need seems to be for more games.	Purchase more games. Ask for donations.	Improved to 5 rating in two weeks after games were purchased.

Figure 6-8

2. Develop evaluation criteria and procedures before program implementation.

3. Provide for ongoing evaluation to take care of program "fix-its" along the way.

4. Develop specific criteria for each program sub-area identified.

5. Provide sufficient evaluation data for the decision-makers to make intelligent decisions.

6. Help determine whether change is economically feasible or whether it will make any difference.

7. Make provisions, where applicable, for large scale parent, student, teacher and administrator involvement.

8. Take into consideration personnel expertise and other resource limitations.

9. Be flexible enough to be easily revised or modified.

10. Be simple enough for everyone to understand and use.

Evaluation models to be effective need to be developed separately for general and specific program use.

[3] John Frank, Jr., *Complete Guide to Co-curricular Programs and Activities for the Middle Grades* (West Nyack, N.Y.: Parker Publishing Co., Inc., 1976), pp. 249–50.
[4] Ibid.

7

Evaluating Obective-

Based Instructional Programs

Education is rapidly approaching an era where the public is emphasizing the need for accountability. The demand for "Back to the Basics" reflects, to an extent, the fact that our school curriculum and other school programs have been developed in such an unorthodox fashion that they may not be meeting the needs of students. To whom should the school be accountable? The taxpayer, P.T.A.'s, pressure groups, politicians, state legislatures, parents and any number of other groups feel that the school has an obligation to be accountable to them. How do we develop instructional programs that can be properly evaluated to insure a measure of accountability?

New instructional programs must be developed that will meet the needs of all students. Programs should provide substantial outgrowth beyond the basics, up to and including comprehensive academic activities for gifted students. Newly designed instructional programs need to include a built-in evaluation process to ascertain whether program expectations are being met.

Evaluation of any instructional program precludes that the initial planning phase of that program has, as its focus, the following major question: *What does the school expect the instructional program to include?*

An example used by the Memorial Middle School in White River Jct., Vermont, follows:

1. The instructional program should have as one component a priority or basic objective phase.

2. Phase two should spell out accelerated instructional objectives and insure that students are afforded the opportunity to progress at their own rate beyond the priority or basic objective stage.

3. Provisions in phase three should include an objective program designed to provide relevant experiences for gifted and talented students.

Once the school has established what it believes is its ideal instructional program, it should develop an action plan-evaluation model. This model must include expected end results in terms of the ideal instructional program desired for the school, an action plan to reach desired results, a time-frame evaluation for field testing and evaluating the progress of the program and, finally, provisions for switching gears once evaluation shows procedures are failing.

Unlike many models that chronologically list the means to the end, this model suggests that the school start with what is not happening now and what should be occurring in the future!

The three phase instructional objective program has been plugged into this model because this author feels it is the best in-

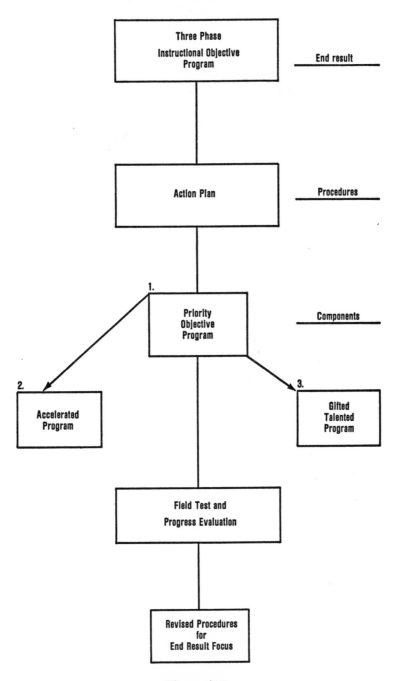

Figure 7-1

123

structional program that any school can design. Other programs can readily be fitted to this model and evaluation methods established.

DESIGNING THE ACTION PLAN

Step Two in the model suggests that an action plan be developed which will facilitate the adoption, planning, development, implementation and continual evaluation of the program. Continual program validation can be accomplished within the action plan by:

1. Developing a time-frame progress plan.
2. Involving the total staff in the field test evaluation process and subsequent revisions.

The time-frame progress plan should spell out exactly where and when each component of the three phase or any other instructional program will be at specified times. This process allows the total staff to monitor progress and measure development. A typical time-frame progress plan might be constructed similar to the following:

Memorial Middle School

Time-Frame Progress Plan

School Years 19XX-XY

1. Arithmetic *Priority Instructional Objectives* now operational fifth through the eighth grade will be expanded to include Phase II *accelerated objectives*. Phase II accelerated objectives will be field-tested from December to June and will be revised during a summer workshop. Initial work on Phase III *Enrichment Objectives* shall begin during the summer workshop of 19XX.
2. Social Studies and Science *Priority Instructional Objectives* will be developed and articulated 5-8 by June 19XX. A summer curriculum committee will correlate, revise, modify, etc., and put into written form a working

set of basic skill objectives and a corresponding Student Profile Chart for use in September 19XX. Initial work on Phase II *Accelerated Objectives* will begin the summer of 19XX and follow the pattern as outlined for Math implementation.

3. English-Reading *Basic Skill Objectives* recently completed will be field-tested and validated during the 19XX-XY school year. Necessary revisions and modifications will be made to establish a fully operational program for the 19XX-XY school year.

Preliminary copies of Phase II *Accelerated Objectives* should be developed and ready for the summer curriculum committee to correlate into a workshop model. It is expected that Phase III *Enrichment Objectives* will follow the pattern of arithmetic with initial work taking place during the summer of 19XY.

4. Music, Art, Physical Education and all other subject areas will develop and articulate basic skill objectives 5-8 by June 19XX. It is anticipated that these areas will be able to develop a corresponding Student Profile Chart for use in September 19XX. Further development of Phase II Accelerated and Phase III Enrichment Objectives will be planned for use in September 19XX.

It is important that we follow the above target dates closely so that our work coincides with planned district priority objective coordination goals set for September 19XY.

Figure 7-2

The successful implementation of any action plan denotes the need to involve teachers and utilize their continual input.

STAFF INVOLVEMENT–AN EVALUATION TOOL

Involving the total professional staff in the formulation, implementation and evaluation of the instructional based objective program is of paramount importance. With the advent of mandated competency-based education came a growing resistance by teacher organizations toward any program that dealt with measurable behavioral objectives. Teachers and administrators who have had this competency-based instructional concept imposed upon them by state legislatures and districts employing commercial firms are often justified in their resistance.

Many programs have been implemented without proper planning, resource allocation, or *evaluation procedures* established. Often schools fail to consult teachers on what learning objectives should take place at various grade levels or how to evaluate the success of stated objectives.

It is this author's belief that although programs can be mandated to teachers, you cannot dictate their success. Only when teachers and other administrators have had a part in the development, implementation and continuous evaluation of instructional programs designed to meet local school needs will they be successful.

A program designed to involve staff should:

- Insure that all teachers are represented continuously and that everyone participates when necessary and/or practical.

- Insure that each person is comfortable that his or her observations and judgments will be taken into account (are important).

- Focus on improving programs rather than simply judging them.

- Create a decision-model that clarifies different types of decisions and helps insure that everyone has a stake in making timely and accurate data availabe when appropriate.

Evaluation that comes from those involved in the action, when built into the proper decision making model, will pay continual dividends for any school instructional program.

EVALUATING THE PRIORITY INSTRUCTIONAL OBJECTIVES PROGRAM

Phase I

What do we believe children need to learn? How do we identify basic competency objectives? At what grade levels should we teach certain basic competency skills and how do we evaluate mastery? How do we develop articulation for our school and coordinate these with district objectives?

These and many other pertinent questions should be addressed by every school seeking to properly prepare children for their roles in society. The following memo establishes a frame of reference for developing priority objectives that can readily be evaluated:

Memo:
To: Middle school teachers and administrators
From: Donald Fox, Principal
Subject: Priority Objectives—Phase I

It is imperative that we establish minimum levels of expectations for students. In terms of priority objectives, we must determine what students *need* to learn in order to function in society. In an era of accountability, we must be able to show that we can and do accomplish what we claim.

A percentage of students, because of severe learning disabilities, socio-economic deficiencies, emotional problems, and other variable factors, will not meet all levels of established competencies. We cannot pretend that school is a cure-all for society's ills. For some students no program will be sufficient. However, we must present evaluative data to justify non-attainment of minimum levels of expectations. By establishing priority skill objectives for students, we also establish an on-going and continual evaluation process.

Minimum levels of expectations should not be constrictive and self-limiting for students. The instructional program should foster advanced competency skills to insure continued creative student development.

Below you will find an example of priority basic competency objectives used in another school. I offer these as samples. We should be thinking of objectives for our own children.

I hope this information will be helpful for our first workshop meeting October 1.

Figure 7-3

PRIORITY INSTRUCTIONAL OBJECTIVES

(Sample)

Grade 1

Language Arts

1. When given a list of one syllable words, the child will demonstrate his knowledge of long and short vowels by saying them correctly seventy-five percent of the time.
2. Given a word, either vocally or visually, the child will locate the given letters, consonants, blends, and diagraphs by correctly decoding it seventy-five percent of the time.
3. Given material geared to his ability, the child will be able to reconstruct in his own words what he has read.
4. Given material geared to his ability, the child will read fluently and with expression.
5. Given the opportunity to go to the library and select his own materials, the child will demonstrate his need to read for pleasure and information by quietly reading the selected book.
6. After being presented with a list of sight words geared to his ability, the child will state orally each word with eighty percent accuracy.

7. Given paper and pencil, the child will write his first and last name correctly.
8. Given paper and pencil, the child will legibly write the alphabet.
9. Given an example to copy, the child will be able to reproduce it by the third attempt.
10. Given a one step direction, the child will carry it out effectively.
11. Given a picture, the child will be able to construct a story orally from its contents.
12. Given stories, records, or tapes the child will demonstrate his ability to listen attentively for a minimum of 10 minutes.
13. Given a written selection, the child will be able to recognize a period, question mark and be able to express orally what they mean.

Figure 7-4

The priority objectives listed in Figure 7-4 have a built-in evaluation tool. Some measure of skill attainment needs to be stated within the objective itself. The literature is replete with the fundamentals of objective construction, and it is not necessary to focus on this area. For our purposes, we have found that the common denominator for a practical objective contains two essential elements:

1. The condition should be stated—given a list, written selection, blank map, word problem, etc. the student will—

2. The measurement process should be identified—state orally each word with eighty percent accuracy, recognize a period, question mark, name the countries, solve the problem, etc.

Objectives should be designed so that when a grade level list is formulated, eighty percent of a student's progress can be evaluated within the scope of the normal student-learning process. The objectives should not focus on testing, but rather they should be conceived as a learning tool for the teacher. When objectives become test-oriented, the tendency is to teach to the test situation and the normal student-learning process is altered. Methods of measuring and recording student progress will be discussed in Chapter 8.

VERIFYING ACCELERATED LEARNING PROGRESS

The purpose and intent of accelerated skill objectives is to insure that students are offered opportunities to proceed beyond priority objective levels to a point that is commensurate with their ability.

Accelerated skill objectives should make provisions for exploration and investigation of subject matter equal to a student's ability to experience success. While the need to evaluate progress still exists, it need not be as formidable a task as is necessary with priority objectives. Consequently, accelerated objectives should be written to describe what the child will do but not necessarily how well he will do it. Evaluation should focus on the adequacy of accelerated objectives and how well students are handling those objectives.

Where grading and other measurability factors are of paramount importance, objectives may be written to include measurement components similar to priority skill objectives. Overemphasis on measuring progress within the total instructional program can lead to skill saturation at the expense of the humanistic approach. Accountability for the purpose of identifying what children should learn is healthy; overdone, it can be deleterious to the student-learning process. Measured behavior is not always evidence of learning, and overemphasis on specific learning can lead to an ignorance of complex learning opportunities. Balance in a program is crucial.

The following sample teacher instruction sheet was designed for use with Figure 7-5, Accelerated Objectives.

Phase II Accelerated Objectives
Arithmetic Guidelines K-4

The list of topics under phase two is intended as a supplementary list of concepts to which the teacher might expose the student after he has achieved mastery of all of the items in the basic list of behavioral objectives. In general, the teacher should not use a topic from the phase two list until a student has a thorough knowledge of each concept from the list of behavioral objectives for his grade and all preceding grades. An exception may be made in the case where a phase two topic could be used to clarify, introduce, or provide readiness for a topic in the list of behavioral objectives for that grade. The emphasis should be on exposure, and evaluation should focus on this area rather than mastery. However, students who are capable of mastering a particular concept should be encouraged to do so. Some procedure for evaluation and record keeping should be developed for these students.

The attached list of proposed phase two objectives is just that—a proposal. It has been compiled for the purpose of having a list of topics which can be used as a basis for discussion in preparing a list suitable for use in our school. As you read through the attached list of proposed topics for phase two, it is suggested that you evaluate each item in terms of its suitability for your students. Record inappropriate items so that you will be prepared to make your contribution to the creation of a revised list. Keep in mind that the following types of changes are possible:

1. Add items to the list.
2. Delete items from the list.
3. Change an item from one grade level to another.
4. Renumber the items for a grade level so as to change the priority of items.
5. Move some of the ungraded items into a particular grade level.

PROPOSED   OBJECTIVES   FOR   PHASE   TWO—
ARITHMETIC

Accelerated Objectives

(Partial listing)

(Subject to revision after further consideration and discussion.)

GRADE 1
1. Given manipulative aids such as popsicle sticks, some in bundles of ten, the student will explore place value of 2 digit whole numbers.
2. Given physical aids such as fraction pies or drawings, the student will explore the meaning of the term one-half (used orally as a part of a whole).
3. Given groups of objects or symbols on paper, the student will explore the meaning of a *set* of objects.

GRADE 2
1. Given several 2 digit whole numbers, the student will experience the task of writing them in expanded notation.
2. The student will practice renaming a 2 digit whole number (e.g., $32 = 20 + 12$) using physical aids or exercises on paper.
3. Given manipulative aids such as popsicle sticks, some in bundles of ten, some in bundles of one hundred, the student will explore place value of 3 digit whole numbers.
4. Given an addition example written in horizontal form using the + symbol, the student will practice setting it up in the usual vertical form for addition.
5. Given word problems appropriate for the second grade, the student will practice both a) determining the operation(s) to use and b) finding the solution.
6. The student will practice reading the symbol ½ cor-

*We recently evaluated our Fountain Valley management system and found it was living up to our expectations. The central office has approved our continued use of this program.

*The school evaluation group will conduct a revised evaluation of the Fountain Valley program this May.

WRITING/SPELLING

1. *Highest ratings by staff* (on a scale of 4)
   Merrill Spelling for Writing (2.6)
   Learnco *Spellmaster* (2.5)

2. *Recommendations*

   *The *Merrill Spelling for Writing* has been recommended for our school, based on a concensus of other elementary school evaluations in the district.

   *A time line for implementation will be designed this summer by a committee yet to be selected.

   *A refinement of the management components of this program should be accomplished during the summer of 19XX.

   *Procedures for evaluating student writing samples based on the New Canaan Model should be added to the writing section of the curriculum guide. Training should begin for our staff and other schools who have adopted this program in the summer of 19XX. We should prepare for implementation of system-wide procedures for evaluating writing samples at all schools during the 19XY–XZ school year.

3. *Rationale*

   The *Merrill Spelling for Writing* program integrates spelling and written composition. It contains word lists based on frequency of use at each level. The format and activities provide for a structured writing program. By adding New Canaan Evaluative criteria (via writing sample procedures), we would have a complete writing program.

Figure 7-10

The procedure described above encompasses two key elements of a total instructional materials selection process. It identifies school needs and provides for involvement of the teachers and administrators in the materials evaluation and selection process.

SUMMARY

This chapter has focused on the three phase instructional objective program and the *Action Plan Evaluation Model* designed to provide a built-in evaluation process. We have discussed the evaluation process for:

1. Priority instructional objectives.
2. Accelerated instructional objectives.
3. Enrichment (gifted) instructional objectives.

Pertinent to the success of any objective based instructional program is the evaluation process designed to insure grade level articulation. The most successful instructional-based objective programs are those that are designed, implemented, and evaluated at the local level by local staff personnel. This is especially true when you evaluate and select materials for use in the instructional program.

Measuring Student 8

Progress

What program design does your school have for measuring student progress? Have your teachers received adequate training in measurement techniques? Do all teachers follow prescribed procedures when measuring student progress? Surprisingly, many schools do not have a student measurement program designed to effectively determine how well students are doing. No specific program is best—each school must develop a program that will meet its own particular needs. This chapter will highlight some important student measurement program considerations.

PREPARING TEACHERS TO MEASURE STUDENT PROGRESS

Too often school administrators assume that teachers have been adequately trained in the art of measuring student progress efficiently and effectively. The chances are that few teachers have acquired sufficient skills in this area unless the school or district has conducted inservice sessions in the past. Most teachers practice methods that have been passed on to them from others or utilize methods that they have developed themselves out of necessity. The fact that a school operates without a design for measuring student progress may, in itself, be deleterious to the orderly process of student learning.

Inservice programs for teachers are a must for any school that expects to do a first-class job in measuring student progress. Teachers must learn how to develop methods of assessing student progress based upon established objectives, use assessment data to develop a planned sequence of learning activities and interpret progress to the student and his parents.

Inservice programs should focus on a systematic approach toward providing a consistent method of evaluating daily progress. Teachers should be expected to acquire skills in the areas of pre- and post-testing, standardized tests, criterion tests, test construction, self-assessment, diagnostic testing, observation techniques, interview assessment and any number of other measurement tools.

How does the administrator determine what training is most needed? School administrators may determine what training teachers need by several methods such as asking teachers to submit suggestions, conducting question and answer interviews, giving teachers a test or making their own observation judgments. While all of the above may work, each has its own limitations. One highly successful approach is to have teachers anonymously provide their own data for the decision makers through a definition and rating exercise.

MEASURING STUDENT PROGRESS

(Definition and Rating Sheet)

Purpose: This exercise is designed to help you and the administration identify the areas most in need of further inservice training. We are only interested in what you as a group know and feel collectively. You should *not* identify yourself.

Directions: Define each term listed below in two or three sentences. Be specific as possible. When you have finished the definitions on the right hand side of this sheet, list in order of importance those terms you are in need of learning more about.

Terms: Ratings
1. Criterion Testing   1.
2. Teacher-made tests   2.
3. Individualized grading   3.
4. Informal tests   4.
5. Standardized tests   5.
6. Observation measurement   6.
7. Test construction   7.
8. Interview assessment   8.
9. Diagnostic testing   9.
10. Self-assessment   10.

Figure 8-1

Another somewhat similar approach that may be utilized is to give your teachers a test at a faculty meeting and allow them to keep the test while you seek their input for training needs based on what happened when they took the test. This method provides teachers with clearer insights into their own deficiencies and usu-

ally creates a better understanding of the need for further training. A sample test might look like this.

Teachers Test #3

MEASURING STUDENT PROGRESS

Directions: Define the first term listed and explain its relationship and use with each second term listed.
1. I.Q. Norms—Expectancy Levels
2. Standard achievement tests—Base data comparison
3. Criterion reference tests—Priority objectives
4. Pupil profile analysis chart—prescriptive instruction
Part Two
List the method you use most to measure student progress. In 25 words or less defend this approach over
other available methods.

Figure 8-2

SURVEYING SCHOOL MEASUREMENT METHODS

How does your school measure student progress? Do you
know how many standardized tests are being used in your school?
Criterion referenced tests? Other measurement tools? It is essential that each school examine and understand where they are and
what they are presently doing with student measurement before
they can determine where they would like to be in the future.

The school evaluation committee should compile various
measuring techniques used by the school and utilize the data collected as a base for determining future measurement programs. A
sample approach to compiling the necessary information is displayed in Figure 8-3.

Similar charts or displays can be developed by the evaluation
team for criterion referenced tests, profile charts, department
tests and other measurement tools used in the school. A composite
of all student measurement procedures will help the decision-
makers in their planning for a comprehensive student progress
measurement program.

Standardized Tests Used at
Hartford High School

Name of Test	Purpose of Test	Cost per Student	Administrative Time	Teacher Evaluation
Career Planning Program dev. by ACT-Houghton Mifflin, 1973	Career Guidance	$1.82/student Test materials and scoring Service	2 hrs.	Good
ACS-NSTA Coop Amer. Chem. Society Univ. of So. Florida	Part of final exam in Chemistry	$1.00/student	80 min.	Very Good
Home Ec. Tests Home Ec. Pub. Sheldon, Wis.	Classroom testing with-in course	.20/student		Good
Paul Pimsleur French Proficiency Test - 1967 Harcourt, Brace	Part of final exam and group placement with-in class	$25 for tapes purchased in 1967		Very Good
*English Coop Educ. Testing Service Pub. 1960	Program Eval. and Individual Diagnosis	Cost of IBM answer sheets (700)	1½ hrs.	Very Good
*Coop Tests Algebra I Algebra II Trig. Geometry	Program Eval. Part of final exam	.06/student Answer sheets only	1 hr Geom.- 2 hrs.	Fair to Good
Arith. Proficiency Test-locally developed, local norms	Placement of 9th graders into Basic Math or Algebra I		1½ hours	

Note: Although these are all standardized tests and have national norms, the norms are not always used in the individual student evaluation.
*Indicates where norm is used.

Figure 8-3

EVALUATING SCHOOL MEASUREMENT METHODS

Once measurement programs have been established, it is important to constantly evaluate them based upon previously stated goals and objectives. It is important that both the skills to be measured and the method used to measure student progress be evaluated. The sample evaluation questionnaire that follows was designed to determine how valid certain established behavioral learning objectives were and how well teachers rated the pupil progress profile used to measure student progress. A sample student progress profile appears later in this chapter.

Basic Behavioral Objectives—Pupil Progress Profile

Mathematics Evaluation Sheet #2

1. Indicate the grade level you teach.   ____

2. (a) Did most of your students acquire mastery of each item on the list of the basic behavioral objectives *for your grade level?*   Yes ____ No ____

   (b) If not, list the objective number (e.g., 3.6 for grade 3, objective 6) for each objective which your students did not master.

   _____

   _____

   _____

3. (a) Have all of your students secured mastery of each item on the list of the basic behavioral objectives for *grade levels below yours?*

                                            Yes ____ No ____

   (b) If not, list the objective number for each objective which your students did not master.

   _____

   _____

   _____

4. (a) Did any of your students work on basic behavior objectives for grade levels above yours? Yes ____ No ____

(b) If so, list the objective number for each such objective which any of your students worked on.

_____

_____

_____

5. (a) Did any of your students work on objectives from the list of PROPOSED OBJECTIVES FOR PHASE TWO?

Yes ___ No ___

(b) If so, list the objective number or the name of the topic which any student worked on.

_____

_____

_____

6. Once a student has mastered the basic objectives for his grade level, which, in your opinion, should he be assigned to do?

(a) basic objectives for the next grade level, or

(b) phase two accelerated objectives?

_____

_____

PLEASE ANSWER THE FOLLOWING QUESTIONS EITHER ON BACK OR ATTACH ANOTHER SHEET OF PAPER.

7. Make any recommendations you have for changes, additions, or deletions in the list of basic behavioral objectives for your grade level.

8. Make any recommendations you have for changes, additions, or deletions to the pupil progress measurement profile.

9. Has the pupil progress measurement profile proved to be a valuable measurement tool?   Yes ___ No ___
If no has been checked, please tell us why.

Figure 8-4

TESTING, HOW MUCH AND FOR WHAT?

This author recently visited a number of schools throughout the country and discovered that testing is often viewed as either essential or deleterious to the instructional process. Many school testing programs I observed fell somewhere between the two ends of the spectrum. One New York State school tested students continuously. Every time a sub-unit was completed, students were given a test based upon previously prescribed objectives, the tests were sent downstairs to a computer to be scored and the results returned the same day. Students appeared to be well-indoctrinated and adapted to this type of measurement process. Another mid-western school utilized only teacher-made tests and had not used standardized or criterion referenced tests for two years.

Somewhere between these two philosophies, the question: "How much testing and for what?" can be answered. Testing can and should be an important part of the instructional process. When overdone, testing detracts from that process by robbing students of valuable instructional time. Properly integrated within the total instructional program, testing can provide valuable data for:

1. Students to measure their own progress.
2. Teachers to revise or modify programs to meet student needs.
3. Decision-makers to evaluate programs.

Each school must develop a testing program that is based on its own particular needs. As a general guideline, the measurement of student progress should take place within the confines of the classroom and should be an integral part of the daily instructional process. Testing should be a supplementary phase of measurement used to validate other measurement activities. Schools should not succumb to outside pressures to test only what standardized tests will measure; they must also find ways to measure a student's ability to think, analyze, socialize, learn from experiences and function in society. In today's world, these may be as necessary for survival as pure mastery of academic skills.

DETERMINING SCHOOL EXPECTANCY LEVELS

The validity of any school testing-program depends on several factors including the expectancy level of students being tested. Achievement tests have limited value if they cannot be compared to what students can be expected to accomplish. Developing an expectancy level for any group of students presents certain problems, foremost of which involves the use of I.Q. tests. I.Q. tests, though quite controversial, are one means of determining expectancy levels for school use. Specifically used as base data for comparison purposes, I.Q. tests can be utilized as a valuable measuring tool. If the average I.Q. of a seventh grade class is 100 and the class is tested for math computation skills at the beginning of the school year, the average class achievement score should test out a 7.0. Similar results should be expected with similar smaller groups with different I.Q. readings. When expectations don't match up with actual achievement scores, a discrepancy exists which may have implications for the instructional program. When this condition exists, it is a signal for the school to evaluate further the results to determine if, indeed, a problem exists.

The student progress profile may be a more valid and acceptable means of determining school expectancy-levels. The profile designed to record a student's attainment of specific grade-level skills based upon established instructional objectives (see Chapter 7), provides up-to-date comparison data. The student progress profile also shows actual levels of ability in terms of performance rather than projected levels of ability which have to be derived from I.Q. scores. When standardized achievement scores are compared with profile results, a more accurate analysis of any existing discrepancy occurs.

Teacher-rating and other variables may be used to predict group expectancy, but the I.Q. and progress profile methods offer a more efficient and reliable approach. A graphic display of expectancy and achievement data appears in Figure 8-5.

The concept of establishing school expectancy levels has

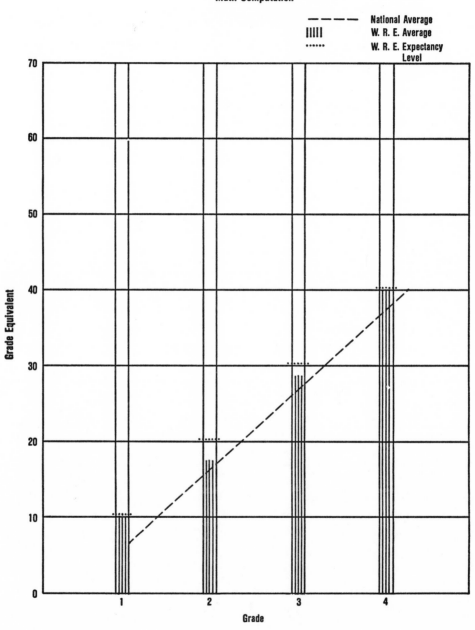

Figure 8-5

proven beneficial in a number of schools. Your school may wish to consider such an approach or you may prefer to focus on the criterion evaluation process.

DEVELOPING CRITERION EVALUATION PROCEDURES

The true measure of a student's progress lies not in what he can do compared to others but what progress he makes toward accomplishing prescribed objectives. The criterion approach to measuring student progress insures that a student will be evaluated based on individual performance rather than some comparison with national norm scores.

Every school should have as a basic goal—less dependency on standardized tests and more on criterion evaluation techniques. Standardized tests need not be excluded but should be used as back-up data for performance measurement, based upon established instructional criteria.

It is important that schools develop appropriate criterion tests to adequately measure student progress; however, it is not necessary to spend a disproportionate amount of time developing an elaborate testing system. Tests are only one way to measure a student's performance against specified tasks and other means such as the use of the classroom profile and alternative assessment approaches may be more effective. Alternative approaches may include specially designed games, duplicated materials and hands-on manipulative materials.

Many evaluators have already made the criterion approach to evaluation seem so technical that the average administrator is reluctant to be involved. If school administrators have to develop expertise with the likes of DRT's, DAD's and other such acronyms that professional evaluators have created, very little time will be left to do other administrative tasks. Each school should develop a criterion measurement model that will meet its particular needs. The following model may be modified or revised to meet many of those needs.

The most practical and perhaps successful criterion measurement program is the one that incorporates its operation with the classroom instructional process and utilizes the teacher's ability through daily observation to carry it out. The criterion evaluation approach may be limited to measuring only basic competency skills or it may be utilized almost exclusively to measure progress and prescribe instructional assignments for a year's course work. An example of this approach used by an upstate New York school is shown in Figure 8-7.

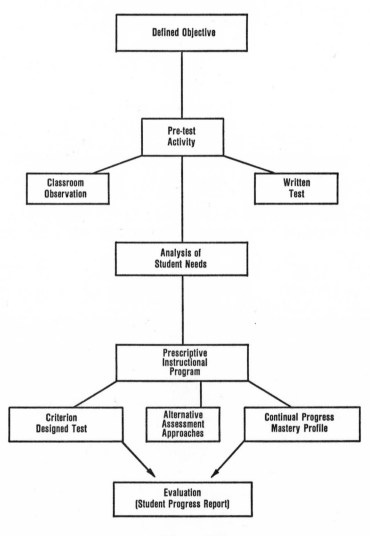

CRITERION MEASUREMENT MODEL

Figure 8-6

MATH CAM - LEVEL 3

PRESCRIPTION FOR: & - &

The Cam Math Test results show that you should work on the following objectives:

Number	Title	Sources	Text	Workbook	Ditto
01	Place Value	Adwes	38-41 A27-38	11	6
		Homif	20-21	8	6
		Coprs			P 1-15
02	Complete the Counting	Adwes	38-39, A 35-40		
		Homif	11,14,15	5-7	
03	Compare Sizes of Numbers Using and	Adwes	42-43 A 39-40		9
		Homif 113,141	5,15,18,89	3	2,5
		Coprs			P-4,17,26 P3-16,18 20 P 4-13
04	Finding of Addends	Adwes	54-57,B5-8		11
		Homif	30,50,51		7,15

Figure 8-7

In the above case, all math work is based on mastering stated objectives for the total course. Students are given periodic tests which are sent to the computer for scoring. The computer then prescribes what work the student needs to do based upon the objective problems he missed. The printout also informs the student where he can locate materials to practice those objectives he did not do correctly. Perhaps somewhere between criterion measurement for basic skills and the sophisticated computor program · described above lies a program for your school!

VALIDATING RESULTS WITH STANDARDIZED TESTS

Most school administrators know what standardized achievement tests are going to say before they are given. So why give them? Do they tell us how to improve childrens' skills? It is not the purpose of this book to argue the merits or shortcomings of the standardized test but only to answer to the extent possible the above questions.

Standardized tests do have a use in the total school student-measurement process when placed in the proper perspective and used with discretion to validate criterion-measurement results. If criterion-measurement analysis leads a school to believe that youngsters are below expectations in the area of reading comprehension, a standardized reading test may be administered and the results compared to criterion data to determine if the standardized test bears out the criterion analysis.

Let's assume that students as a group scored high on reading vocabulary but much lower in comprehension. The results would bear out the original concern that reading comprehension skills were not up to par. This assumption may be oversimplified; yet, it serves as an example of how the standardized test may be used by schools with some degree of validity. While the standardized test does not in this case answer our original question (Do they tell us how to improve childrens' skills?), it does, however, provide the school with concrete data which shows that there is a need to improve childrens' skills in reading comprehension.

Confronted with data from two sources which shows that attention has to be given to upgrading the instructional process in reading comprehension, the school is now in a position to move in that direction.

RECORDING AND REPORTING CONTINUAL PROGRESS

Equally important as the methods developed for measuring student progress are the procedures established for recording and reporting student progress. Schools need to develop recording and reporting approaches that go beyond the report card sent home to parents four times a year.

Individualized instruction, continual progress and even back-to-the-basics programs require more effective ways of record keeping. Reporting procedures both to students and parents need to be improved. Some form of a pupil progress profile is essential for recording performance measured against established criteria. The profile provides a relatively accurate record for displaying student progress, and it can be used effectively to report on a student's performance at any time during the school year.

The profile in Figure 8-8 was designed to record student performance based on selected skill objectives. The numbers to the right indicate the number of the objective and also indicate the grade level of the objective. The numbers to the left signify state basic competency objectives that correspond to local objectives listed on the right. This type of profile is valuable because it provides an ongoing record from elementary through high school.

EXPLORING ALTERNATIVE EVALUATION APPROACHES

Student progress evaluation cannot be a sometime thing; it must be a continuous daily exercise built into the instructional process. Our schools, through inservice sessions, must explore alternative approaches to measuring student progress within the classroom learning environment. What are the ways to measure student progress other than standardized achievement tests, criterion-references tests and teacher-made end of the unit tests? The list shown in Figure 8-9, by no means complete, offers a few suggestions.

NAME: _____

LAST   FIRST   MI

Fill in appropriate grade level above succeeding columns.
Unless a student fails, numbers would proceed: 1, 2, 3, 4, etc.

I. READING

A. Ability to pronounce words

5	1. Long & Short Vowels	[3.3]
2.5	2. Letters, Consonants, Blends	[1.2][3.4]
2.3.5	3. Sight Words	[3.2]
5	4. Roots, Prefixes, Suffixes	[4.2]
2.5	5. Dolch List	[3.2]
6	6. Dictionary Pronunciation	[4.1]

B. Ability to Read Orally

1.3.4	1. Statements & Questions	[2.1]
8	2. End Punctuation	[3.1]
1.8	3. Phrasing & Punctuation	[4.1]
1.8	4. Play Participation	[7.1]
1.8	5. Oral Reading	[8.1]

C. Ability to Read Independently

1	1. Reads Pleasure Material	[2.1]
1.6	2. Reads Self-Selected Material	[5.1]
1.4.6	3. Silent Reading	[5.2]
4.6.7	4. Information Materials	[8.1]

D. Reading Comprehension

7	1. Sentence Sequence	[3.1]
7	2. Main & Supporting Idea	[4.1]
7.T2	3. Comprehension Questions	[4.2]
7.+T6	4. Order of Events	[6.1]
5.6	5. Vocabulary & Word Usage	[7.1]
7.T10	6. Fact & Opinion	[9.1]

Figure 8-8

1. *Self Evaluation*	Example: Children can be given quizzes, check-off assignments and other progress type activities to correct or record themselves. Children may evaluate their own progress when involved in contract instruction. This is where we agreed you would be—where are you?
2. *Observation Checklist*	Example: For each unit, the teacher develops her own progress checklist that she can use on a daily basis in the classroom. Through constant observation, the checklist can be filled in for each student. Time should be allotted during class, between classes, during preparation period or after school each day to insure that observations are recorded while they are still vivid in the teacher's mind.
3. *Performance Graphing*	Example: Twenty math skills are listed by degrees of difficulty. Each member of a class of 20 is listed and as each student acquires a skill, his/her progress is plotted on the graph. The graph allows the teacher to measure progress for all students on one piece of paper and it provides an instant feedback mechanism.
4. *Interview*	Example: In order to determine how well each student has mastered the skills required to do research, a teacher sets up interviews with each student and asks him/her to recite the proper procedures he/she will use when doing his/her own assigned research project.

5. *Teacher's Diary*	Example: Teacher X has one class working on contract assignments. He decides that one way to keep track of daily progress is to record the happenings of each class period. Since students have different contracts for varying lengths of time, this approach will help teacher X identify where students are, and it will provide a ready document for future reference.
6. *Specific Documentation*	Example: All faculty members decide that certain criteria constitute an acceptable written paragraph expected of all students. Samples of a student's writing are filed and progress is measured against the accepted school criteria.
7. *Situational Tests*	Example: The goal of the automotive course is to provide sufficient skills so that each student will be placed in an automotive job. The instructor and prospective employer evaluate each student's skill level. Employment becomes the ultimate measure of progress and the number employed out of the total class denotes overall student body progress.

Figure 8-9

SUMMARY

Measurement inservice programs for teachers are a must for any school that expects to do a first-rate job in measuring student progress. In your school you should:

1. Survey present school measurement methods.
2. Evaluate present school measurement methods.

3. Develop a testing program based on your needs.

4. Determine your school expectancy levels.

Criterion evaluation techniques provide an alternative or supplementary approach to the standardized test. Your school should develop a criterion measurement model that will meet your particular needs. Standardized tests play an important role in the total program when they are used to validate criterion measurement results.

Standard procedures should be established for recording and reporting student progress, and we recommend the pupil progress profile as the best tool available. Several alternative measurement approaches may be utilized including: self-evaluation, observation checklist, performance graphing, interview, diary, specific documentation and situational tests.

Designing Effective

9

Staff Evaluation Programs

One essential prerequisite to effective staff evaluation includes the involvement of the total staff in designing the evaluation process. When teachers participate in the planning stages of the evaluation program, they are more apt to look upon evaluation as a positive experience and feel less threatened by it.

COOPERATIVELY DESIGNED JOB DESCRIPTIONS

Where collective bargaining contracts permit, cooperatively developed job descriptions should be established for all staff positions within the school. Job descriptions developed between teachers and administrators provide for an evaluation framework from which each can initially identify areas that need to be evaluated. A job description helps to eliminate much of the ambiguity and misunderstanding that often arises when staff evaluation takes place. Specific stated duties provide teachers with an understanding of what they are expected to do. How they are expected to do it can be determined by the teacher and the administrator who is responsible for the evaluation.

Job descriptions should include at least the following three performance categories:

1. Instructional
2. Managerial
3. Professional

Other categories may be added based upon individual school needs, i.e., co-curricular and extra-curricular. The job description below represents one example.

TITLE: THE PRIMARY LEARNING CENTER
JOB DESCRIPTION

The role of the Primary Learning Center teacher:

Provide enrichment experiences for the children in Kindergarten through Grade Three particularly in the areas of science and math. The atmosphere of the center should be one which nurtures the natural curiosity of young children. The teacher reports directly to the principal of the school.

PERFORMANCE RESPONSIBILITIES

A. *INSTRUCTIONAL:*
1. Provides experiences that promote the learning of scientific process skills.
2. Serves to enable the primary unit to further refine its individualized approach to learning.
3. Organizes and implements a supplemental math program.

4. Creates a rapport with children which is supportive of the learning process.
5. Provides opportunity for use of manipulative materials.
6. Utilizes a variety of instructional materials and activities.
7. Encourages a positive self-image by acceptance of each child's observations.

B. *MANAGERIAL:*
1. Maintains a Science-skill Profile for each child.
2. Establishes a visually stimulating environment for the study of science and math.
3. Develops reasonable rules of behavior within an atmosphere of exploration and discovery.
4. Obtains and uses materials as needed to carry out the program.
5. Schedules and meets classes at designated times.
6. Develops adequate plans for substitutes.
7. Takes necessary safety precautions with laboratory equipment.

C. *PROFESSIONAL:*
1. Keeps classroom teachers aware of areas of study.
2. Follows Board of Education policies and administrative rules and regulations.
3. Continues professional growth and is aware of current educational trends.
4. Establishes and maintains good relationships with parents and the community in promoting the educational program.

DEFINING EVALUATION RESPONSIBILITIES

Effective staff evaluation requires that a clear statement be made defining who will be responsible for what area(s) of evaluation. The larger the school, the greater the need to define evaluation roles. A careful delineation of responsibilities helps the designated evaluator to develop expertise in his assigned area of responsibility, and it makes it clear to teachers who will be evaluating them.

The memo statement below displays how these responsibilities might be defined at the high school level.

TO: Anyone's high school staff
FROM: P. Jones
SUBJECT: Evaluation and Supervision
DATE: December 16

There is little argument that evaluation and supervision should have as primary goals: the improvement of instruction, the maintenance of sound procedures of pupil supervision and accounting that contribute to a good school environment, and self-improvement of the individual teacher.

Recent deliberations of administrators and department heads have resulted in an approach to provide a better opportunity to accomplish the above goals in a more satisfactory manner.

Department Heads will be primarily concerned with teacher performance, teaching techniques, providing learning experiences which carry out the school philosophy, general departmental objectives and specific course objectives, and teacher attitude which contributes positively to the total atmosphere of the school.

Housemasters will be primarily concerned with teacher performance in the following areas: pupil supervision (study halls, cafeteria and related assignments); pupil accounting (attendance and tardiness); teacher techniques and effectiveness in dealing with students (behavioral and disciplinary problems); and teacher attitudes which contribute positively to the total atmosphere of the school.

The principal will be concerned with overall evaluation and assessment of teacher performance and effectiveness.

There is no intent to imply here that some areas of primary evaluation responsibilities do not overlap administrative personnel. It is not possible to separate these concerns into components all of the time. However, concentration of evaluation efforts aimed at certain important objectives should create a more cohesive situation for all concerned.

Figure 9-1

PERFORMANCE GOAL SETTING AND MEASUREMENT TECHNIQUES

The foremost goal of staff evaluation should be to provide individuals with constructive feedback which will allow them to improve the quality of instruction they offer. The best chances of success for meeting this goal occur when the designated evaluator and staff member sit down and develop a set of goals and objectives that each can agree are important for that individual. The process may call for some negotiation if both parties cannot agree as is often the case. This process does not negate an administrator's right to insist on specific goals where staff deficiencies are pronounced.

This procedure can be expedited if a standardized worksheet is developed and used by everyone in the school. The evaluator should fill out one goal and objective worksheet and the evaluee another and these should be used during goal-setting conferences (displayed in the time schedule section). A goal and objective worksheet might look like this:

Evaluation Goal and
Objective Worksheet

Introduction: This worksheet has been designed by the school evaluation committee as a tool to upgrade the staff evaluation program. You are asked to fill in as completely as possible the areas listed below. You should have this prepared and ready for your first meeting with your designated evaluator. Your evaluator will have a similar sheet filled out for you.

1. Develop 5 goals for your area of responsibility.
   A. Rank these goals high-low in order of impor-
      tance. Highest Lowest
                 1   5
2. List a minimum of two objectives in measurable terms
   for each goal chosen.
   A. Where possible relate these to designated school
      goals.
3. Develop a time schedule for goal-objective accomplishment.

Figure 9-2

The evaluation goal and objective worksheet should lead into
a conference agreement on at least three goals and the appropriate number of objectives necessary to insure goal success, including an agreed to time schedule for accomplishment.

Evaluation Goals and Objectives for _____

Year 19 ___ 19 ___

1. Goals to achieve
   A.
   B.
   C.
   Others
2. Objectives in measurable terms. Specify goal letters
   after each.
3. Time schedule agreed to.

Signed _____
Evaluator

Signed _____
Teacher

Figure 9-3

SELF-EVALUATION, A NECESSARY INGREDIENT

One of the most effective tools utilized in improving the quality of teaching is the administering of a self-evaluation. The self-evaluation allows a teacher to look at his own performance in relationship to the success of his students. A concerned teacher will welcome the opportunity to explore his strengths and weaknesses without the threat of administrative involvement.

Self-evaluations need to be an integral part of the total staff evaluation program. They should be mandatory, but the teacher should be allowed to choose the type of evaluation he wishes to use and the results need not be shared with the administration.

Name _____

Self-Evaluation Instruction Sheet

In addition to our formalized evaluation program, each member of the staff will produce evidence of doing a self-evaluation. The options could be, but are not limited to:

1. Video-tape of a classroom situation to be critiqued by the teacher or his/her peers, or
2. A written self-evaluation pointing out strengths and areas to exert effort to change, or
3. A classroom visit by a peer, i.e., a teacher from our own system or from another system, or
4. A teacher self-evaluation questionnaire form— option of form numbers 1, 2 or 3, or
5. Conduct a student evaluation of performance by means of interviews or student evaluation questionnaires, or
6. An evaluation diary on daily performance kept for a period not to exceed five weeks but not less than three, or
7. Completion of the Meagher Teacher Competency Skills checklist, or
8. Other (explain)

The only evidence of completion you need to submit is this sheet with the information filled in below. If you wish to share your experiences with your regular evaluator, please do!

"I, _____, participated in a self-evaluation
         teacher name
process this year. The process I used was _____ ".

                                    Date _____

Figure 9-4

ESTABLISHING TIME SCHEDULES FOR EVALUATION

It is important to record and display exact time sequences for the staff evaluation program. A complete and detailed time schedule will help to avoid misunderstandings and allow everyone to work from the same base of reference.

(Sample)

On or Before	Beginning or Probationary Teacher	On or Before	Experienced Teacher
Sept. 21	First observation	June 15	Ensuing year goal development
Sept. 27	First conference and goal setting conference		
Oct. 15	Second observation— if problems noted above		
Dec. 1	Second observation— first rating on form: "Observations #1"	Dec. 15	First observation
		Dec. 22	First observation and goal review conference
Dec. 7	Second goal setting and adjustment conference		
Jan. 15 to February 15	Follow-up evaluation as needed.	Feb. 15	Second observation if needed—revision of goals if necessary.

March 3	Informal self-evalu-ation discussion	
May 15	Self-evaluation report due	
June 1	Ensuing year goal development con-ference	June 10 Self-evaluation report due

Figure 9-5

Continued use of the time schedule will necessitate some review and revision on the part of the staff and administration. Changes that are made cooperatively are most always the most effective.

PROVIDING PROVISIONS FOR SELF-IMPROVEMENT

No staff evaluation program is complete unless it allows for and encourages self-improvement based on evaluation needs. It is not always possible for a teacher to correct certain deficiencies identified by the evaluation process without inhouse provisions for continual staff development and improvement activities. You should assume a leadership role in developing a school inservice program that goes beyond district offerings. Methods of identifying teacher inservice needs and the selection of appropriate activities to meet those needs have to be explored. Several of these activities include visitations, inhouse staff instruction, inschool workshops, outside workshops, professional journals and other individual approaches.

A continual program needs to be developed to identify inservice progress and needs. The *Inservice Needs Survey Sheet* is one way to start.

Inservice Needs Survey Sheet

1. Based on your own goal and objective evaluation, what areas do you feel should be added to our priority inservice list this year?

    A.

    B.

    C.

    D.

    E.

2. How could these areas best be covered? Example: Workshops, demonstrations, etc.

    A.

    B.

    C.

3. Would you be willing to offer your services to conduct a workshop in a particular area if it is identified? _____ If so, state the area. _____

4. The following skill areas have been mentioned as possible common areas in which people might need to improve their competencies. Please fill in the squares below:

	High Interest	Some Interest	Low Interest
1. Grouping for instruction	___	___	___
2. Reading in the content area	___	___	___
3. Contract Instruction	___	___	___
4. Behavior modification	___	___	___
5. Teaching the basics	___	___	___
6. Testing	___	___	___
7. Recording progress	___	___	___
8. Other ideas, suggestions, concerns or whatever	___	___	___

Figure 9-6

A strong self-improvement program combined with a well-developed self-evaluation component of the staff evaluation program produces highly motivated and effective teachers. It is also important to decide who should evaluate the principal.

Conducting

10

The Evaluation

Once the target for evaluation has been identified, it is important to determine how the evaluation will be implemented. This chapter will highlight some of the more important aspects to consider when conducting your school evaluation.

HOW TO CONSTRUCT THE EVALUATION TIME CALENDAR

It is important that all school personnel be aware of and understand when and how the evaluation will be implemented. If an evaluation is to be conducted over any extended period of time, a time calendar should be developed and distributed to all school personnel. The time calendar might look similar to the following.

Time Calendar—Writing Skills Competency Evaluation

Pre-test, Grade 8   September 27
Ongoing Instructional Evaluation   October 1 thru March 1
   A. Reports due January 1, February 1
      and final reports March 1
Periodic Testing Evaluations   January 3 and February 27
Data Collation and Analysis   March 1
Decision on Program Revisions   March 5
Final Post Test   June 14
Evaluation Report and Recommendations   June 22

Figure 10-1

A yearly evaluation time calendar for instructional programs helps to integrate evaluation into the total instructional process.

COORDINATING EVALUATION WITH THE TEACHING-LEARNING PROCESS

Much of the negative attitude expressed toward evaluation results from the fact that it is often too far removed from the classroom and those who work with children. Teachers view evaluation as something decreed from above and something that has to be done, "So let's do it and get it over with." This attitude is hardly conducive to achieving the main goal of evaluation— improvement of the quality of instruction.

Whenever possible, evaluations should be designed and conducted to coincide with the teaching-learning process. Evaluations conducted using only pre and post tests or other scheduled written measurement devices leave something to be desired. Where possible, evaluations should be conducted that will allow teachers and other selected personnel to collect data without undue interruption of the instructional process.

One way to insure that a portion of the evaluation will be conducted within the teaching-learning environment is to develop evaluation devices that call for data to be collected from the day-to-day instructional operation.

Example: (Goal)	Eighty percent of students in the eighth grade will improve their writing skills to meet proficiency levels prescribed for Grade 8 by March 1.
(Evaluation)	English teachers will record those students who meet the prescribed level while engaged in the English writing unit. All other subject teachers will establish proficiency through examination of a minimum of three written assignments. (Reports, essay answers to questions, etc.)
(Instructions)	All subject area teachers should send their list of students who have reached the prescribed proficiency level to the English department head once a month starting January 1.

The evaluation for the above-stated goal becomes an ongoing activity that can be handled within the confines of the classroom without undue disruption of the instructional process. A teacher does not have to have extensive evaluation training to conduct the evaluation effectively. Evaluation conducted in this manner need not be done at the exclusion of other evaluation procedures. Certainly, your school may wish to have all students take a written test at a given time to verify or dispute classroom evaluation results. It is important that evaluation not be something that is always divorced from the daily instructional scene. Evaluation is most effective when it is conducted as an integral part of the instructional process rather than a "tack on" to it.

THE PRINCIPAL'S CHECKLIST

The school principal or his designee is responsible for overseeing the school evaluation program. Essentially provisions need to be made to insure that the who, what, where, when and hows are accounted for. The principal's checklist provides a handy method of checking both the preparation for conducting the evaluation and the progress of the evaluation throughout its various stages.

Principal's Evaluation Checklist

____ Responsibility for carrying out the evaluation has been established.

____ Agreement has been reached on the parties to be evaluated.

____ Data to be collected has been identified and plans made for collecting it are ready.

____ Evaluation methods have been agreed upon and the necessary resources allocated.

____ Teachers and other personnel involved in the evaluation have received the necessary inservice training.

____ The evaluation time calendar has been delivered to all school personnel.

____ Provisions have been made for analyzing the data collected.

____ A date has been established to deliver evaluation results to the decision-maker.

____ Recommendations have been requested with evaluation results.

____ Reporting procedures have been established.

____ Provisions have been made to test the validity of the evaluation itself.

Figure 10-2

Other criteria may be added to your checklist or you may wish to expand the checklist concept by developing a more detailed descriptive operations guideline.

COLLECTING EVALUATION DATA

Probably no aspect of evaluation is more important than data collection and its subsequent use as evidence for decision-making.

A number of built-in constraints such as negative staff attitudes, politics, resource limitations and lack of external support all have to be overcome to insure effective data collection. Many of these constraints can be eliminated or decreased when teachers are actively involved as members of the school evaluation team. A number of data collection do's and don't's appear below.

Do's and Dont's

DO

Make sure that competent people are assigned to collect data.

Provide adequate resources to insure that proper collection of the data takes place.

Make sure that sufficient data is collected to insure a valid evaluation.

Use more than one tool to collect your data, i.e., interviews, observations, questionnaires, etc.

Include enough of a target population to insure credibility to the data collected.

Develop a standard or expectation to compare data with.

Establish provisions for collating the data periodically when the collection process occurs over an extended period of time.

Develop a comprehensive data recording system.

DON'T

Collect so much data that it creates confusion and becomes waste material.

Collect data without a detailed plan of action.

Involve more people in the collection effort than is necesary.

Use highly technical terms that will confuse participants.

Ignore built-in individual school constraints.

GETTING PERSONNEL TO CONDUCT THE EVALUATION

A number of options appear when an administrator asks the question, "Whom do I have conduct the evaluation?" When school evaluation teams are responsible for conducting evaluations, no problem exists, but where no one has been previously designated, the problem becomes more acute. Teachers often see evaluation as a threat and one way to eliminate this constraint is to involve teachers in the conducting process. The more a teacher is allowed to participate and have a say in how the evaluation should be conducted, the less the threat appears to be. The administrator has the option of assigning staff or seeking volunteers. The latter, of course, is the preferred option. A third, but less desirable option is to have other personnel from the district conduct the evaluation or go outside and hire an external evaluator.

Some of the possibilities include:

1. Teachers conduct their own evaluation.

2. Teachers conduct the evaluation cooperatively, sharing responsibilities.

3. The principal and one or two others may conduct the evaluation.

4. Some group from the central office may be responsible.

5. The university consultant or some outside agency may be enlisted.

A SAMPLE IN-SCHOOL EVALUATION

To: Chairman of the Evaluation Committee
From: Math Evaluation Sub-committee
Subject: Fifth grade math program—evaluation procedure

Overview	—All of our fifth grade students enter the middle school from five elementary schools. Each elementary school follows the same prescribed instructional process and basic competency skill expectations are the same at all schools. Our task was to determine what percentage of students enter grade five achieving at grade level in math.
Evaluated (Who)	—All fifth grade students were tested with the exception of four students.
(When)	—The second week of school in September. Students who were absent testing day were given make up tests the 12th and 14th day of September.
(How)	—We used the Stanford Achievement Test, Math Skills Criteron Reference Test #4 and Math Profile Charts were examined.

—Teachers administered the tests and examined the profile charts with assistance from the three member math evaluation sub-committee.

—The data collected was analyzed and interpreted by the evaluation sub-committee.

Preparation

—All fifth grade teachers attended a two hour workshop to familiarize themselves with the task at hand. The workshop was held during a pre-school orientation session Friday 10 A.M. to 12 P.M.

—Stanford tests were purchased this summer and the Criterion Reference Test was given to teachers before school was dismissed in June.

—All fourth grade math profile charts were given to homeroom teachers the first day of orientation.

—Students were given a special test orientation session on the ninth of September.

Results

—Only seventy-six percent of the students achieved at grade level as identified by all three evaluation instruments. The lowest percentage was measured by the Stanford Achievement Test where only sixty-eight percent were at grade level. Students scored highest on the Math Profile Charts—eighty-three and one-half percent (83.5%).

Problems

—The evaluation math sub-committee felt that the Stanford Achievement Test did not measure a number of items our children had been taught and in several cases asked questions not identified on our basic competency skill list. We are unsure how to go about reconciling differences between district skills taught and those measured by the test.

Reporting

—All results have been graphed for display purposes. A statistical report is attached to this memo.

Recommendations

—This sub-committee feels that the evaluation committee should recommend to the principal further study of district basic competency skills for the expressed purpose of verifying their validity.

—All three instruments pointed out a pronounced weakness in computational skills. The math coordinator should study this data thoroughly and may wish to involve district personnel from each elementary school in an effort to upgrade this deficiency.

Figure 10-3

Figure 10-3 shows one approach to involving school personnel in the evaluation process. Teachers administered and examined test results and the committee followed through to produce the finished product.

INTERPRETING EVALUATION DATA

Professional evaluators probably would argue that interpreting data is not the same as analyzing data and each should be a separate step. In an effort to consolidate and simplify the evaluation process for the practicing school administrator, the two will be intertwined.

The first step in analyzing and interpreting data should be to determine if the data is complete. Next, several questions should be resolved. Does the data provide answers to original evaluation questions asked? If not, the total data collecting process should be reviewed to determine if faulty data collection caused the problem. What factors or variables could have thrown the data off and changed the reliability of the evaluation data? If the data answers original evaluation questions, is it conclusive enough to justify program changes?

School administrators often get bogged down trying to work with technical evaluation activities such as mean, average, standard deviation, etc. The major goal of the interpretation process should be to develop an understanding of whether the program just evaluated lived up to its established goals and objectives—if not, why not?

If groups of students are evaluated, the interpreter should look for two signals:

1. Significantly higher scores may show that the new program apparently is effective and probably should be continued and/or expanded.

2. Excessively higher scores probably should be looked upon with suspicion until further study indicates the validity of the data.

After evaluation data has been analyzed and interpreted, the appointed decision-makers must determine how appropriate their conclusions are, based on the effect they may have on the total school operation. Then they must ascertain whether implied changes will conflict with previously evaluated school programs.

REPORTING EVALUATION RESULTS

How you publish evaluation results depends on who is going to utilize the report. It is important that everyone affected by the evaluation be appraised of results in clear and concise terms. Publishing evaluation data and making it available to everyone helps take away some of the ambiguity and mistrust often associated with evaluation. It is better for everyone to have information to work with (even if it is not positive) than to have none at all.

Some guidelines for reporting evaluation results:

1. Keep sophisticated evaluation terminology to a minimum.
2. Provide a clear explanation for any symbols you use.
3. Provide a glossary of these terms actually used.
4. Make the report fit the evaluation—use graphs, charts and other displays when appropriate.
5. The report should speak specifically to the purpose of the evaluation and relate to program goals and objectives.

How comprehensive should the report be? There is no magic answer to this question; as a general rule the report should be equal to the complexity and scope of the evaluaton conducted. Evaluation reports may show specific data or they may relate to a general overall report of a program. The following sample reports show both approaches.

STUDENT EVALUATION
of the
RIDGE LEARNING CENTER

YES		NO
374	Do you like this year's Learning Center program?	42
325	Do you like having visitors in the Learning Center?	86
214	Have you gotten to use the Learning Center as much as you would like?	104
236	Do you like Interest Study better than working on subject areas for self-improvement?	124*
164	Do you like the idea of being sent from your math class to do math or from reading class to do reading?	97*
292	Would you like to know what you will be studying before it comes up in your classes so you can learn about it in advance in the Learning Center?	55*
305	Do you find the Goal Cards helpful to you?	109
333	Have you gotten as much help as you would like?	87
351	Does Miss Glasser seem to understand what is important to you?	62
374	Do you think your teacher likes the Learning Center?	42
373	Do you like making up your own mind about what materials you will use?	47
253	Do you behave better in the Learning Center than in your homeroom?	98 (*)
242	Do you think this year's Learning Center program has helped you to improve more than last year's program?	67

412   Have you answered these questions honestly   8
       and carefully?
       What ways could the Learning Center be im-
       proved?

_____

_____

422 first-fifth graders responded.
*59 first graders were not asked these questions.
(*)Upon request of the first-grade teachers, this question
read: Do you behave the same in the Learning Center as you
do in your classroom?[1]

Figure 10-4

The specific data evaluation displayed in Figure 10-4 provides a definitive measurement process which is readily identifiable to the reader. The evaluation summary is usually more subjective.

THE EVALUATION SUMMARY

The principal should be responsible for producing an evaluation summary of the total program at the end of the school year.
This summary should be based on a series of short-term evaluations and any long-term studies that have transpired. The evaluation summary should include the following criteria: student response to the program, teacher attitude and performance, effect
on the total school operation, and parent-community reaction to
the activity program. A typical evaluation summary might look
something like this:

1. The majority of students have expressed positive attitudes
   toward the activity program. Student questionnaire and
   conference evaluations show that all but a few activities
   are highly popular. There is considerable evidence to

_____

[1]Joyce Fern Glasser, *The Elementary School Learning Center for Independent
Study* (West Nyack, N.Y.: Parker Publishing Co., Inc., 1971), pp. 181–82.

show that student participation has been at an all-time high and, with the addition of several new activities, will remain so. Studies show that students have assumed greater responsibility for planning and evaluating their own exploration experiences. The only significant negative aspect of the program seems to be our inability to offer all students their first choice.

2. There has been a significant change in teacher attitude toward the activity program. Initially, there was significant concern among staff members about the program. Concern centered around our ability to provide a sufficient number of activities to make the program successful. The teacher survey shows that we have removed all doubts, and practice has shown that many new activities have originated from the teachers. Administrative evaluation shows that there has been considerable carryover from the activity program into regular academic program by teachers. A good part of the hands-on methodology used in the activity program is now being applied to academic areas and increased student productivity appears to be evident.

3. The effect of the activity program on the total operation of the school shows that the general tone of the building has improved tremendously. Vandalism has been drastically reduced, absenteeism has been down significantly, and morale as of this date rates at an all-time high.

4. Parent-community support for the program has been about ninety-eight percent favorable. Approximately two percent feel that this program is a "frill," and that we ought to get back to the basics. Parents remain, in most cases, our best public relations people, and have helped to promote the program. Newspaper and radio coverage of the program has been very positive, and student presentations to our local service organizations have met with tremendous success. Our eight parent instructors not only rate the program very highly but have also done a tre-

mendous job of promoting the activity program to friends and neighbors.[2]

DECISION-MAKING BASED ON EVALUATION

Evaluation is beneficial only when it provides essential information to decision-makers for the expressed purpose of improving school effectiveness. Designated decision-makers need to receive ongoing evaluation data through the monitoring process. Constant examination, overseeing, revising, adapting, adopting and modifying must transpire before a viable judgement can take place. Only then can the decision-maker assume that any activity is achieving the quality kinds of outcomes it is supposed to achieve.

Essentially evaluation data should provide the decision-maker with several possible options. Such options might show that:

1. There is no significant difference between what existed before and unless further study proves otherwise, the school should maintain its present operation with an eye toward continual improvement.

2. Certain modifications to the evaluated program will be needed if it is going to continue to operate.

3. The program has been successful and evaluation data indicates that the program should be expanded.

4. The program has not accomplished stated goals and objectives and evidence indicates that modifications or revisions will make no significant difference. The program should be abandoned.

5. There is not enough evaluation data available to make a valid decision on the program at this time. Either additional evaluation will be necessary or judgments will have to be made without the benefit of evaluation results.

---

[2]John Frank, Jr., *Complete Guide to Co-curricular Programs and Activities for the Middle Grades* (West Nyack, N.Y.: Parker Publishing Co., Inc., 1976), pp. 243–44.

REVIEWING THE EVALUATION

Decisions should not be considered final until a thorough review of the evaluation has been conducted. Each school should
develop its own method of determining whether the evaluation
used to make decisions was in fact a reliable evaluation. Was the
evaluation carried out according to prescribed procedures? Are
there any doubts about the evaluation? These questions and
others need to be asked and answered to the decision-maker's
satisfaction before he can put his stamp of approval on it and proceed with decision implementation.

SUMMARY

The evaluation time calendar is an essential part of any ongoing program and should be developed so that it is coordinated
with the total teaching-learning process. Two important tools to
consider when conducting the evaluation include the principal's
checklist and a do's and dont's list.

Basic questions that need to be resolved include:

1. Who is going to conduct the evaluation? (In-school evaluation team preferred)
2. What criteria will be used to interpret evaluation data?
3. How will we report evaluation results?

Evaluation data should provide essential information necessary for decision-makers to make valid judgements. No decisions
should be considered final until a thorough review of the evaluation has been conducted. It then becomes necessary to discover
whether the evaluation is reliable.

Exploring 11

External Evaluation Possibilities

Inhouse evaluation offers the most effective and efficient approach to school evaluation. External evaluation should not be considered as a substitute for, or equal to, a well-planned and implemented internal evaluation. The external evaluator, too, often is here today and gone tomorrow, offering evaluation findings but no proposed solutions. The external evaluation does, however, have its merits. The evaluation team or local evaluation department often develops blind spots from working too closely to the daily operation. The outside evaluator who comes in with a different perspective may identify hidden mistakes. Secondly, the external evaluation can serve as a verification of local evaluation efforts which may be necessary to add credibility in the eyes of the public.

USING PROFESSIONAL EVALUATORS

The most common resource bank of experts in educational evaluation come from the colleges and universities. Another excellent source is larger school districts that employ evaluation specialists. In some cases even private agencies may supply the necessary expertise. When considering hiring a professional evaluator, the following questions should be satisfactorily answered:

1. Have we established that an expert is needed?
2. How much of an evaluator's time do we need?
3. What portion of the evaluation can we do ourselves?
4. Is the right evaluator available?
5. Do we have the time and staff to work with the professional?
6. What are our financial constraints?

Few schools can afford to hire a professional evaluator for an extended period of time or for too many evaluations. Where can the professional be used most effectively? The least costly and most practical use of the professional evaluator may be to evaluate proposed school program plans. A planned school program should be reviewed by someone who can evaluate the design and proposed operation of the program. The professional evaluator may discover potential pitfalls in the program before implementation begins. Shortcomings are best discovered before action begins when only trial and error may produce evaluation data. The following excerpts were taken from an evaluation of a proposed middle school health education program designed to include sex education. Only the negative portion of the report has been retained to emphasize how incomplete the evaluator found the program plan.

Evaluation Shortcomings

Sound principles of program planning and implementation dictate that certain guideline criteria be followed. The criteria are:

#1 Program development should result from a *comprehensive* needs assessment program designed to ascertain the desires of the community:

Point: I find no evidence in this document that such a needs assessment was carried out. This leads me to question the validity of content.

A. Needs assessment should seek out all members of the community who will be involved in the program: i.e., staff, parents, administration, students, and other taxpayers. Public meetings alone do not constitute a viable school needs assessment.

#2 Once the assessment process verifies the need for program development, a state of intent, purpose, goal or similar description should be formulated and agreed to:

Point: I find no evidence this was done and consequently would not be able to make any judgment as to whether proposed inputs could equal projected outputs because I find *no statement of agreed intent.*

#3 Long-range objectives, short-range objectives and action plans to insure continuity and articulation (K-12) should be developed:

Point: I find no evidence that this process has transpired. Page 2: *Prologue* appears to leave it wide open. "Latitude to teach," is fine, but it offers no assurance that all students will be offered any continuity or articulation of instruction. The prologue appears to offer an escape clause for accountability provisions.

#4 Specific program content objectives should be developed and *process* objectives designed to insure desired attainment:

Point: I find no process objectives in the document I
         have studied.

#5   Resource allocation procedures should be clearly de-
     fined:
     Point: I find reference to a number of material type
              resources, but few or none pertaining to staff,
              facilities, money and other resources needed
              to specifically insure estimated benefits to the
              child.

#6   A built-in evaluation system should be an integral part
     of any program development process. The evaluation
     process should be continuous and provisions should be
     made for recycling when evaluation shows desired out-
     comes are not being attained:
     Point: No evaluation plan seems to be in evi-
              dence.

Conclusion:

     It would appear that the planning team has done
an extraordinary amount of work on this program
document and the materials and course content proposed are excellent. The involvement of staff and students in the development of this program is commendable. I believe revisions in this program based upon
correcting deficiencies described under evaluation
shortcomings will lead to a successful program in the
future.

                         Biggio Fopp
                         Evaluations Unlimited, Inc.

Figure 11-1

If the professional evaluator is to be used to evaluate an existing school program, several procedures should be adhered to:

1. A contact person should be designated by the school to
   work with the evaluator.

2. A written agreement should be drawn up that specifies
   what is to be evaluated, when and how.

3. The evaluator must know to whom he is to report and
   what type of report is expected.

4. Financial arrangements should be spelled out and provisions made for necessary project resources.

REGIONAL EDUCATION ASSOCIATION EVALUATIONS

School principals, looking for alternative ways to evaluate school programs, may explore utilizing the talents of their own regional principals' association or a similar regional educational organization. Principals' associations are not usually designed to provide evaluation services; however, as the need to evaluate increases and budget allocations decrease, the potential for utilizing services on a regional basis becomes a more viable alternative.

Regional principals' associations can develop a program evaluation model and each principal may agree to serve on evaluation teams on a rotating basis.

THE PARENTS' EVALUATION GROUP

In Chapter 4 we discussed program planning and evaluation teams and the need to have parent representation on these groups. A similar but alternative approach is to create a school evaluation group comprised only of parents. An evaluation group consisting only of parents has several advantages.

- It allows for more parents to participate.
- Parents usually feel more secure with a group of their peers and, therefore, are inclined to be more active participants.
- Evaluation results have a tendency to be more readily accepted by the public.
- It provides additional evaluation data for the school to analyze and compare with other evaluations before making decisions.

As principal, you have to assume a major leadership role in the organization of the parents' evaluation group. Careful attention must be paid to the selection of members. Criteria for selection should include both grade level and geographic representation. You must prepare a written charge to the group and present a suggested method of operation for their consideration. Care must be taken to insure that the group develops sufficient skills to carry out its tasks, but you need to be careful not to give the impression that you or other school personnel are trying to dominate the scene. The watchword needs to be guidance and direction but not imposition.

Because parents are not educators and least of all evaluators, the number of evaluations they should be given responsibility for must be limited. Where possible, the parents' group should be given the task of evaluating programs that were instituted as a result of strong needs assessment data. The parents' evaluation group also can be most effective when they use the total school parent population as their target group for collecting data.

The methods and approaches the group might use conducting its evaluation include neighborhood coffee-hour meetings, telephone interviews, door-to-door interviews, observations and evaluation questionnaires. A parents' survey questionnaire might be used by a parents' evaluation group in all of the methods listed above.

UTILIZING STATE DEPARTMENT OF EDUCATION EXPERTISE

An often unused resource available to schools exists at the State Department of Education level. Too often the only communications between state depatments and local schools transpire as a result of state-mandated programs where department personnel have to evaluate. State departments employ consultants with varying degrees of expertise in all subject areas.

While these consultants may not be expert evaluators, they have the distinct advantage of being able to visit and compare similar programs throughout the state. The ability to compare your program with a number of others throughout the state gives the state consultant a unique evaluation tool not readily available through other means. The Middle School Industrial Arts program evaluation below is an illustration of the type of evaluation available to schools upon request.

STATE OF VERMONT

DEPARTMENT OF EDUCATION

Montpelier

REPORT OF CONSULTANT'S VISIT

School: Hartford Memorial Middle School   Date: October 1977

Person(s) Contacted: Francis Duncan, Principal

Activity: Visitation—Industrial Arts

Division or Areas:

( ) Aerospace	( ) World of Manufacturing
( ) Construction	( ) Materials Testing
( ) Drafting	( ) Metals
( ) Electricity/Electronics	( ) Plastics
( ) General Industrial Arts	(xx) Power Mechanics
( ) Graphics	(xx) Woodworking
( ) World of Construction	(xx) Other Drawing

I. Purpose of Visit: Evaluation

COMMENDATIONS AND RECOMMENDATIONS:

I was disappointed that my time schedule did not allow me to observe the Metals Program at the Memorial Middle School. My observations are based on three phases of the six phase program.

COMMENDATIONS

1. Improvements to date in the lab.
2. Evidence of the organization of course content.
3. Evidence of long-range planning by the teacher in the curriculum and facility area.
4. Willingness of the teacher to develop and work in the new curriculum pursuits.
5. Enthusiasm reported for the new power tech course.
6. The work observed by the principal with low-ability children.

RECOMMENDATIONS

1. Post a clean-up schedule.
2. Post the enclosed safety rules on the machines.
3. A program of testing, student notebooks, and safey handouts should be developed around the Vermont Industrial Arts Safety Manual.

4. Textbooks for metals, power, drawing, and woods should be purchased as soon as possible to be used by the students.

5. More specific assigned projects and activities should be developed which will hopefully result in more progressive content.

6. This year's snowshoe project should be developed around a junior achievement type of theme. This would include organization of a company, sale of stock, job descriptions, mass production of the item, consumer survey, and completely through to liquidation and profit sharing.

To date we are very pleased with the progress made in the program during the past six months. I look forward to a visitation in the spring to see the completed efforts of the maintenance department.

Sincerely,
Sam Cummings   cc: Floyd Rising
Industrial Arts Consultant   Phoebe Fopp
                                  Francis Duncan

Figure 11-2

Evaluations from state department personnel need not always be so formal. You may wish to have informal general observation, thought-sharing visits held periodically.

HOW TO USE THE DISTRICT EVALUATION COMMITTEE

School effectiveness in the future will be dependent in part on a school's ability to reallocate resources based upon evaluation data. To accomplish this task, school districts need to look in the direction of a district evaluation team or committee. Chapter 5 discussed the individual school evaluation team and mentioned briefly the need for district articulation among schools and grade levels. Where school districts such as Birmingham, Michigan, are forward looking with their district-wide evaluation team, it is an easy process to coordinate local school evaluation efforts with those of the district team.

The district evaluation committee can provide a number of evaluation services to individual schools. The possibilities include:

- Planning and conducting an evaluation for the school.
- Helping the school plan and implement an evaluation.
- Providing resource personnel and materials.
- Providing a district-wide evaluation model for all schools to use.
- Designing an evaluation model for a specific school program.
- Conducting follow-up evaluation studies.
- Making recommendations for program modification and revision based on evaluation data analysis.

As an external evaluation source, the district evaluation committee offers a real plus in that it is readily available throughout and after the evaluation. Another plus should occur with improved communications and understanding when local school staff serve on the district evaluation committee.

COMMUNITY EVALUATION QUESTIONNAIRES

Ultimately, the community makes judgments on how effective any school is, and school administrators need to insure that there is ample opportunity for the community to evaluate school programs. Utilizing the community as an external evaluator has two distinct advantages. First, done properly, it provides a sound external evaluation approach. Second, evaluation allows the community an opportunity to have input into school programs and, consequently, is a good public relations mechanism for schools to use.

Unlike a needs assessment questionnaire, the community evaluation questionnaire should focus on previously publicized goals and a specific program designed to reach these goals, i.e., needs assessment indicated that children need to improve reading comprehension. The HELP Reading Program was established three years ago to improve reading comprehension. Does the community evaluate this program as a success?

Community evaluation questionnaires may be designed as follow-ups to previously disseminated literature which outlined to the community the purpose, goals, objectives and procedures of the program.

Prerequisites to community evaluation questionnaires include periodic written dissemination of program philosophy, goals, objectives and other pertinent information. Pre and post conditions attached to the community evaluation questionnaire dictate that careful consideration be given to the number of people asked to respond. The more people involved, the more cumbersome the process becomes. The easiest and most effective use of the community evaluation questionnaire occurs when it is distributed through a random sampling process.

COMMUNITY EVALUATION QUESTIONNAIRE

Program: Open Campus Program

Directions: Based upon program information supplied earlier, please respond to the following questions by circling the number you feel best measures the program's success to date. 1 = Low, 5 = High

1. The materials we sent you helped you understand
    all aspects of the program.   1 2 3 4 5
2. Students have handled their new-found freedom
    well.   1 2 3 4 5
3. Your attitude toward the program now is   1 2 3 4 5
4. Goal attainment could be rated   1 2 3 4 5
5. The program's objectives (5) have been met.   1 2 3 4 5
6. Other people you have talked to feel the program
    rates.   1 2 3 4 5
7. The program should be continued.   1 2 3 4 5
8. If your answer to Number 7 is low, please tell us
    why and list any suggestions you have for improv-
    ing the program.

Figure 11-3

Whether by questionnaire or some other method, you should be sure to involve the community somewhere in your overall school evaluation process.

HOW TO USE THE VISITORS' OBSERVATION FORM

Visitors can be used to good advantage as evaluators through the use of the visitor observation form. Parents, professionals and other community members can be invited periodically to observe programs in action and respond to a written set of observations. Other visitors to the building may be encouraged to spend an extra few minutes to fill out the observation form also.

The observation form should focus on a central theme whenever possible, i.e., individualized instruction for all children. A parents' observation form might look like this.

PARENTS' OBSERVATION FORM

Individualized Instruction

To Visitors: We are attempting to provide each child with an individual program that will offer instruction based upon individual student needs. The statements below represent important ingredients of a good program.

Directions: Please check the most appropriate line based upon your observation. Mark only the ones that you are able to observe.

Usually Quite often Occasionally Almost never

___ ___ ___ ___ 1. Children work with a variety of materials.

___ ___ ___ ___ 2. The teacher works with individual children and small groups.

___ ___ ___ ___ 3. Not everyone is doing the same thing.

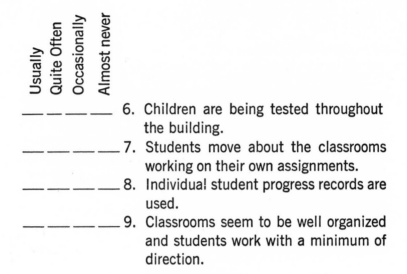

Usually Quite Often Occasionally Almost never

_ _ _ _ 6. Children are being tested throughout the building.

_ _ _ _ 7. Students move about the classrooms working on their own assignments.

_ _ _ _ 8. Individual student progress records are used.

_ _ _ _ 9. Classrooms seem to be well organized and students work with a minimum of direction.

Figure 11-4

The parents' observations form is most effective when parents have been thoroughly informed about the program prior to being asked to use the form. It is helpful to discover how well parents and other community members know what you are doing in school. Thus, it is beneficial to have an evaluation plan to find out.

SUMMARY

The external evaluation cannot take the place of a good internal evaluation, but it often helps to discover inhouse mistakes and will add credibility in the eyes of the public. The least costly and most practical use of the professional evaluator may be to evaluate proposed school program plans before they are put into operation.

Outside evaluation groups that may be used by your school include: regional education associations, parents' evaluation teams, state department of education consultants and the district evaluation committee.

The *Community Evaluation Questionnaire* and the *Parent's Observation Form* are two methods that may be employed to insure that the public has an ample opportunity to evaluate your school.

Evaluating 12

The Missing Links

After all is said and done, it really hasn't been! School evaluation is an ongoing, never-ending process that needs to be reviewed periodically throughout the course of each school year. Provisions must be made to evaluate all school operations on a priority time-frame basis. Obviously, no school is going to be able to evaluate every single identifiable operation each year. Therefore, long-range plans need to be developed to evaluate missing components over a specific time-frame. This chapter will focus on some of the missing links that need to be evaluated in an effective school.

DEVELOPING A TOTAL EVALUATION RECORD CHART

In Chapter One we illustrated the principal's checklist for identifying activities to be evaluated. Assuming that your school makes provisions for adding to that list, the next logical step should be to develop an evaluation record chart. The purpose of the evaluation record chart is to provide you, the principal, and the evaluation committee with a continual updated picture of where evaluation has been, is now and where it needs to go. All identified activities to be evaluated should be listed down the outside column of the chart, the months of the year on top and years listed at the bottom. A sample evaluation chart is shown in Figure 12-1.

The evaluation record chart should be placed on a wall in the space allocated to the evaluation committee as discussed in Chapter Five. As new areas in need of evaluation are identified, they may be added to the chart. When a new area is identified for evaluation, it is important to plot on the chart when it will be evaluated and if no evaluation form is available, one should be developed.

SCHOOL MAINTENANCE AND UPKEEP

Effective schools are by-products of a number of successful operations. Rarely will you find a highly effective school that does not have a sound maintenance and upkeep operation. Does your school measure up to others? Do you have any evaluation program for determining how well your school is kept clean? How do your teachers rate the upkeep of their rooms, halls, laboratories, lunchroom and other areas of the school? Where do you start the evaluation process?

Because schools are unique and needs vary, there is no set evaluation program that can be adopted by every school. You will need to examine your own situation in terms of responsibility for the total maintenance and upkeep of the building. Where district

EVALUATION RECORD CHART
(Partial Example)

	Jan.	Feb.	Mar.	Apr.	May	June	July	Aug.	Sept.	Oct.	Nov.	Dec.	1980	1981	1982	1983
Class size																
Community needs										EF ✓				✓		✓
Community volunteers						EF ✓							✓	✓	✓	✓
Co-curricular activities											EF (4) ✓		✓	✓	✓	✓
Curriculum development													✓			
Extra-curr. activities														✓		
Educational facilities	EF (State)														✓	
Health services																
Instructional supervision				EF ✓										✓		
Innovative programs					✓								✓			
Instructional materials		✓				✓				✓			✓	✓	✓	
Intramurals			EF ✓			EF ✓							✓	✓	✓	✓
Inservice	✓					✓				✓						
Individualized instruction																
Leadership																
Lunchroom operation					EF ✓								✓		✓	
Library media services	✓											✓		✓		✓
Learning process		EF ✓			EF ✓											

SYMBOLS: EF = Evaluation form prepared
✓ = Denotes month and year scheduled

Figure 12-1

209

personnel such as a director of building and grounds are responsible for certain operations, evaluation efforts will have to be shared; however, you should lead the way in identifying those areas that will need evaluating. A number of the areas to consider are:

1. Custodial operations (overall)
2. Building facilities
3. Building repair
4. Building painting schedules
5. Repair and upkeep of equipment
6. Replacement program
7. Working schedules
8. Working relationships
9. Other _____
10. Other _____

You should develop your own approach to evaluating this area. A series of assessment and evaluation sheets might be developed for each area identified starting with custodial operations.

EVALUATION FORM—NON-PROFESSIONAL PERSONNEL

Teacher Form   *Custodial Operations*

Directions: Please take time to reflect on the following general custodial operations in our building and rate them based upon your own experiences. Check the appropriate column.

	Superior	Above average	Average	Below average	Unsatisfactory
1. How well your own room is cleaned					
2. Custodial working relationships with you					
3. Custodial relationships with all staff					

	Superior	Above average	Average	Below average	Unsatisfactory
4. Custodial working relationships with each other					
5. The condition of the hallways					
6. The condition of the boys' and girls' rooms					
7. The cleanliness and condition of the lunchroom					
8. The condition of all other areas of the building					
9. Please give further information for those numbers you graded below average or unsatisfactory.					
10. Other evaluative insights you would like to share with us in this general area.					

Figure 12-2

Similar evaluation forms may be developed for other areas of maintenance and upkeep. Additional evaluation activities might include faculty discussions, suggestion boxes, custodian self-evaluations, and principal or other administrator evaluations.

At this point, let us examine a number of school operations that need to be considered for evaluating the effectiveness of the total school.

ATHLETICS, INTRAMURALS AND OTHER ACTIVITIES

School-wide activities including athletics and intramurals at the upper grade levels are an integral part of any school operation. School effectiveness is often synonomous with a successful activity program. The school activity program cannot be left to chance; it must have a well-developed and implemented evaluation plan. Provisions should be made to evaluate all aspects of the program. Each individual activity should be evaluated, based upon objectives for the activity and the total program evaluated on previously established goals and objectives.

The activity program should be evaluated by parents, teachers, administrators and students. A sample student evaluation questionnaire follows.

Student Evaluation—
School Activities, Intramurals, Athletics

Directions: Please consider the following statements and rate them from 1-5. 1—High, 5—Low. Circle your choice.

1. This school offers a wide variety of student activities.   1 2 3 4 5
2. The number of activities offered are adequate so all students have an opportunity to participate.   1 2 3 4 5
3. The program is well-organized so that a balance exists between during-school and after-school activities.   1 2 3 4 5
4. Students are offered opportunities to determine what activities should be included in the program.   1 2 3 4 5
5. The types of activities offered meet the needs and interests of the student body.   1 2 3 4 5
6. There is a good balance between athletics, intramurals and other activity opportunities.   1 2 3 4 5
7. Teachers show an interest in the activity program and promote the program to students.   1 2 3 4 5
8. When activities are offered, I am able to get my first choice.   1 2 3 4 5
9. Students are encouraged by the administration and teachers to participate in a number of different activities.   1 2 3 4 5

10. Each student is able to experience success while participating in the activity program.   1 2 3 4 5

11. Our school activity program is well-coordinated with the city recreation program.   1 2 3 4 5

12. If you could, what would you do to improve the total school activity program.
    A. _____
    B. _____
    C. _____
    D _____

Figure 12-3

Similar activity evaluation questionnaires should be designed for parents, administrators and teachers. Specific evaluations for athletics, intramurals and individual activities may be accomplished by this method plus a number of others including observation, group interviews and external evaluations.

STUDENT-FACULTY-ADMINISTRATION OPERATIONS

How often does your school evaluate internal school relationships and operations? Do you know how well students rate the administration? Do students feel that teachers are there to help them? Does the faculty feel united in its efforts?

Internal relationships are usually taken for granted in the overall concept of school operation, and rarely does a school evaluation plan include internal relations as one of its components. This area is extremely important in maintaining the effectiveness of any school and like so many other forgotten areas, is not terribly difficult to evaluate. Methods of evaluating this area include, but should not be limited to, the following: faculty rap sessions, problem identification and remedy suggestion boxes, questionnaires, interviews and external evaluations. A sample faculty evaluation of its own operations follows.

INTERNAL OPERATIONS EVALUATION
(Faculty Operations)

Teacher Form

Directions: Place an X after the term you feel best describes our faculty status at this time. Remember the purpose of this evaluation is to provide data that will be used to improve the overall effectiveness of our school.

1. As a group this faculty has developed a respect for each other and it is in evidence in the daily operation.
   Almost always __ Frequently __ Occasionally __ Rarely __
2. The total school operation is enhanced by the large amount of cooperative planning that takes place among staff.
   Almost always __ Frequently __ Occasionally __ Rarely __
3. Communication flows freely among faculty members and a constant exchange of ideas upgrades the school operation.
   Almost always __ Frequently __ Occasionally __ Rarely __
4. This faculty identifies its own goals and objectives and sets about to accomplish them.
   Almost always __ Frequently __ Occasionally __ Rarely __
5. The need for inservice work and a constant desire to upgrade teaching skills is characteristic of our faculty.
   Almost always __ Frequently __ Occasionally __ Rarely __
6. Continuity is a virtue of this faculty and, as a result, students know what to expect.
   Almost always __ Frequently __ Occasionally __ Rarely __
7. Everyone on this faculty pulls his/her own weight in an attempt to develop a successful school.
   Almost always __ Frequently __ Occasionally __ Rarely __
8. There is a good deal of "esprit de corps" among the total staff.
   Almost always __ Frequently __ Occasionally __ Rarely __
9. If you checked rarely in any of the above, please try to elaborate. You need not involve personalities. Also, what steps might we take to alleviate the condition that exists?
10. What areas did we fail to cover on this form?

Figure 12-4

Similar evaluation forms may be designed for administrative, student and parent operations.

FOOD SERVICE OPERATIONS

A hungry child is not interested in learning, and one who is nutritionally deprived may not be able to learn. Lunch time can be a happy, satisfying time for school children, or it can be just another unpleasant school experience. What kind of conditions exist in your school? Have you ever evaluated the whole food services program to see what part it plays in determining the effectiveness of your school? Some form of evaluation needs to be developed in every school. Several approaches come to mind:

1. Principal-Student lunch—The principal invites several groups of students to eat with him each day for a week. During this time he may ask several questions of students. Do they feel they have enough time to eat? How is the food? Do they get enough to eat? This approach allows the principal to get to know students and conduct an evaluation at the same time.

2. State Department Food Consultant—Invite the State Department of Education to help you evaluate your food services operation. Cooperatively, goals and objectives may be developed which will be useful for future evaluative criteria and the consultant may provide an informal evaluation based on the initial visit.

3. Parents' Questionnaire—Parents are usually ready to give some insights into how well they feel the foods service operation is running. Children most often air their displeasure or satisfaction to their parents concerning the food served, time allotted to eat, lunch lines, eating procedures and other aspects of the program. A brief questionnaire similar to others displayed in this book will help to evaluate the total food services operation.

SCHEDULING PRACTICES

Whether your school is elementary, middle or secondary, the type and quality of scheduling you utilize plays an important role in determining the effectiveness of your school. Scheduling practices range from faculty duty rosters to student schedules and each different practice needs to be evaluated. For purposes of illustration, we will focus on the evaluation of a high school ARENA schedule. The ARENA scheduling process is designed to allow students to actively participate in the selection of their own courses, teachers and times. Immediately following the ARENA scheduling exercise in June, the high school evaluation team conducted an evaluation of the ARENA scheduling operation by gathering data from incoming freshman, Grade 9, 10 and 11 students and teachers involved in the ARENA operation.

Incoming Freshman (Sample)

TO: High School Principal—Mr. Ross
FROM: Evaluation Team
SUBJECT: Grade 8 Arena Scheduling: Student Evaluation
    A questionnaire was administered to 8th graders the day after their experience in the arena. A total of 161 eighth graders responded out of a possible 184. To the question, "Did you like having the opportunity to make up your own schedule and choose your teachers?" 95 said, "Yes, very much," 63 said, "It was okay," and three "Hated it." 141 students felt they received enough help from teachers and counselors before going into the arena; 20 said they did not.
    With regard to the arena itself, the figures are given below and divided into the time of day the students were in the arena (the numbers given are *not* percentages).
    QUESTION: What did you think of the arena experience?

	Morning	*Noon*	*Afternoon*	*Total*
Really good				
No Hassles	56	13	14	83

It was OK	39	9	25	73
I hated it	4	0	1	5

TOTAL 161

QUESTION: Would you recommend that this same procedure be used next year?

	Morning	Noon	Afternoon	Total
Definitely yes	73	20	20	113
I'm not sure	28	8	11	47
Definitely not	0	0	1	1

TOTAL 161

Figure 12-5

It is important to include student comments in this type of evaluation whenever possible. The following written comments were made by students:

1. "It was neat. I felt like I had accomplished a lot when I figured my schedule out. I felt a lot of pride when I got every class I wanted and when I wanted it. It's quite an experience."

2. "I think it was a good experience. I think it taught us a kind of responsibility."

3. "I liked picking your own teachers and class periods. I got almost every teacher I wanted, and class periods were kind of switched around, but it was OK."

4. "I liked being able to pick my own schedule, but when I went to the arena, I had to change all my teachers around. I didn't get any I wanted." (Partial display of comments.)

Comments often provide valuable insights into areas of a program that are in need of improvement or further evaluation.

ARENA SCHEDULING QUESTIONNAIRE

Year of Graduation _____. Please circle one answer for each question.

1. While in the arena, how many period changes did you have to make in your schedule because of closed sec-

tions? (Do not include study halls, lunch or release.)

    (a) none   (b) one   (c) two or more

2. How many courses did you have to drop in the arena? (Do not include Junior Social Studies courses)

    (a) none   (b) one   (c) two   (d) three

3. Are you satisfied with your final schedule? (Refers to periods not courses)

    (a) Yes   (b) No

4. Do you feel the arena method of setting schedules is a good one?

    (a) Yes   (b) No

5. Would you prefer to have your schedule made out by the computer—giving you choice of courses but no choice of teachers or periods? (Release will still be available for those students that the computer has not assigned a course at the beginning or end of the school day.)

    (a) Yes   (b) No

6. Comments:

Figure 12-6

Teacher Response

Teachers were asked to write up their evaluation in narrative form and offer suggestions and recommendations for future scheduling sessions. One unique and somewhat humorous evaluation came back in this form:

"The arena was ascreama
with sparticus I felt abin when trampled in that bin by
lions and beasts and imbibers of the yeast that besot
the brain and quicken the drain.
Seriously tho
The arena created more frustration than satisfaction
particularly among the students. Of all the students
I talked to, none expressed feelings of 'worth it'. I
echo their sentiments. Push the button."

The composite results of the three groups evaluated were mixed and specific recommendations for change were compiled. The evaluation team recommended to the principal that the arena scheduling operation remain in effect for another year and that further evaluation be done at that time.

INSERVICE

How good is your school's inservice program? Do you have a planned inservice program? If so, how do you evaluate the effectiveness of your program? Inservice education, as much as any other component of the total school operation, is responsible for upgrading the effectiveness of a school. Without well co-ordinated evaluation procedures, the inservice program will flounder from lack of direction. Good school inservice programs focus on what teachers like, what they need and the needs of the school. Considering these facts, evaluation tools should be designed to measure those basic goals. Each individual component of the inservice program should have its own evaluation instrument. Some key evaluation methods for inservice activities include:

1. Recording attendance
2. Observing participation
3. Self-appraisals
4. Small group reports
5. Questionnaires
6. Rating objective success
7. Outside evaluators
8. School evaluation committee

A school evaluation instrument for a pre-school orientation inservice program follows.

Inservice Evaluation—Orientation Session

Directions: Place a mark on the line that you feel best describes your evaluation.

	Very high rating	High rating	Average rating	Need to improve
1. Information activities presented by department areas rather than mass faculty meetings.	—	—	—	—
2. The format of Tuesday's lunch, with some informational presentation.	—	—	—	—
3. The amount of time allotted for individual room preparation, etc.	—	—	—	—
Individual Presentations				
4. Math objectives and profiles	—	—	—	—
5. English-Reading objectives and profiles	—	—	—	—
6. Advancement on salary schedule	—	—	—	—
7. Experiential methodology	—	—	—	—
8. Student aide program	—	—	—	—
9. Big sister—big brother program	—	—	—	—
10. Mass immunization	—	—	—	—

11. Which presentation was most valuable to you? _____
12. Which presentation was least valuable to you? _____
13. Are there any suggestions you wish to add that will help us to improve the inservice program?

Figure 12-7

ASSEMBLY PROGRAMS

Evaluation plays an important part in the planning, implementing and revising process of a good ongoing school assembly program. It is important to point out that the scope and depth of the assembly evaluation process should be known and understood by all concerned. To make this task easier, the yearly assembly program should have goals and objectives that are easily evaluated. Each assembly must have established objectives and any evaluation conducted should reflect how well objectives are being met.

Stating Assembly Objectives

1. No less than fifty percent of all assembly programs will be closely tied to the school academic program.

2. The remaining asembly programs should direct their attention to adding new dimensions to student learning.

3. Assembly programs will avoid, where possible, cutting into academic time.

4. Assembly programs should stimulate student interest and provide opportunities for further classroom follow-up.

5. A representative group of the school should be formed to select assembly programs.

Establishing Assembly Evaluation Methods Related to Objectives

1. All assemblies will be evaluated by the assembly committee after each program.

2. Each teacher will be asked to do a formal evaluation using evaluation checklists.

3. Alternative methods may include written student evaluations referring to "likes and dislikes," parent evaluations and homeroom discussions.

4. The district evaluation team will be asked to evaluate the total program once a year.

5. The principal will discuss his overall evaluation with the faculty toward the end of the school year.

SCHOOL MORALE

It may be said that the effectiveness of any school can be measured in proportion to the level of school morale that exists at any given time. School morale—what is it and how do we evaluate it? School morale is, for the most part, determined by the attitudes of teachers, students, parents, administrators and other personnel. A decrease in vandalism, increased teacher initiative and decreased parental concern are all signs of improved school morale.

Since teachers play such a key role in making a school go, evaluation should initially concern itself with teacher attitudes. If evaluation shows that teachers have developed positive attitudes toward their work assignments, then the overall performance of teachers will have an effect on the total school. Teacher attitude surveys are one means of evaluating the morale of the teaching staff. Similar attitude surveys may be developed for parents, students and other school personnel.

A PLAN TO EVALUATE "FIXITS"

"Fixit" items commonly relate to those areas that annoy staff continually, yet are not corrected even though you or another school administrator have the authority to control them. The successful implementation of any school program will be impeded if you have not identified and taken care of the "fixit" items in your school. Next to "fixits," dissatisfaction with salary, fringe benefits and uncontrollable working conditions are the greatest deterrents to positive motivation and increased staff productivity. Thus, administrators must gain expertise in both the diagnosis and remedial process to avoid a continual "fixit" problem.

Evaluation plays an important part in determining which areas can be controlled and which cannot. Efforts should be made continually to evaluate progress in the never-ending task of eliminating outstanding "fixits." Evaluation methods include faculty meetings, evaluation committee investigations, evaluation boxes (similar to suggestion boxes), outside evaluators, and questionnaire forms. A "fixit" evaluation might look like this.

January

"Fixit" Evaluation Form #1

Directions: Please respond to the six areas listed below.
You need not sign your name.

1. Below are the nine "fixit" categories identified at our June meeting in need of action. Please circle only those that you feel are left unresolved.
   a. Sudden schedule changes   f. Time allottments for lunch
   b. P. A. interruptions   g. Input into scheduling
   c. Discipline procedures   h. Open house planning
   d. Planning time   i. Substitute personnel
   e. Equitable staff duties

2. Do you feel the nine above items, at this time, cover all "fixit" concerns?
   Yes ___ No___ If no, what are the others?

3. Do you feel that the administration has taken the appropriate action with regard to "fixit" problems.   Yes___ No___
   If not, what steps do you feel should be taken.

4. Has the evaluation committee developed an evaluation plan for this area that meets with your approval?   Yes___ No___
   If not, what do you suggest for improvements?

5. How often do you feel we need to reidentify our "fixit" needs? Circle one.
   a. Once a year in June
   b. Twice a year—January and June
   c. Three times a year—September, January and June
   d. Other—explain

6. Please add other evaluative insights you feel may help.

Figure 12-8

The format of almost any other evaluation form presented in this book may be modified and adapted to evaluate the "fixit" problem in your school.

SAMPLE EVALUATION INSTRUMENTS

We have mentioned previously that every aspect of the total school operation needs to be evaluated and that nothing should be left to chance. The following evaluation samples indicate how several other school operations might be evaluated.

Field Trip Evaluation

Directions: Please rate the following field trips with a
check (√) and answer the questions below.

	Fair	Good	Very Good	Excellent
1. *Sixth grade trips*				
1. Environmental park				
2. Power plant				
3. Ecological seashore				
4. State legislature				
5. Local court				

2. Which trip most closely adhered to curriculum objectives? _____

3. Which trips do you feel should be continued? _____
   _____
   _____

4. Of the ones not selected, which ones do you feel might
   be upgraded enough to retain—if any?   _____
   _____
   _____

5. How do you rate the conduct of students on these trips?

6. Do you feel the number of field trips is adequate?
   Should there be more or less?
   Adequate____ More____ Less____

7. If the school budget were cut, what priority would you
   give field trips in relation to other activities? Explain
   why.

Figure 12-9

Audio-Visual Use—Evaluation

We would like to determine which pieces of equipment you
find to be most useful to you in the classroom. Please con-

sider your response carefully. Your input will help in determining what purchases we will make in the future. *Place an X in the proper boxes below.*

	Used more than 10 times	Used a few times	Used hardly at all
1. Overhead projector	___	___	___
2. Cassette tape recorder	___	___	___
3. Filmstrip projector	___	___	___
4. Video-tape equipment	___	___	___
5. 16mm projector	___	___	___
6. 8mm projector	___	___	___
7. Opaque projector	___	___	___
8. Instamatic cameras	___	___	___
	___	___	___
9. Record players	___	___	___
10. Slide projector	___	___	___
11. Television	___	___	___
12. Language master	___	___	___
13. Listening centers	___	___	___
14. Small prima viewers	___	___	___
15. Other A-V equipment (specify)	___	___	___
16. Additional information you feel may help to evaluate our A.V. operation.			

Figure 12-10

The type of evaluation instrument you use should be determined by the nature of the activity to be evaluated and the amount of data needed to accurately evaluate that activity.

SUMMARY

The *Evaluation Record Chart* is one practical method that can be used to keep track of what areas still need to be evaluated. Some of the important areas often missed by school evaluation programs are: school maintenance, athletics, intramurals, activities, internal operations, food service program, schedules, inservice, assembly programs, school morale and fix-its. Additional areas to be considered include field trips, audio-visual use and any number of others that your school may identify.

Allocating School Resources

13

Based on Evaluation Data

Increased demands for accountability and diminishing school budgets will necessitate improved procedures for allocating school resources.Principals and other administrators will have to learn to make do with resources available to them. Schools are going to have to show how they are utilizing their resources to maximum advantage. Resources will have to be redirected to areas where they will do the most good for everyone and no longer will schools be able to allocate dollars to support programs that do not provide increased quality. Enter evaluation!

227

UPGRADING SCHEDULING PRACTICES

The average school resource bank consists of ninety-seven percent fixed budget costs and three percent flexibility. Most of the flexibility available to a principal lies in the school's master schedule. It represents your true ability to manuver limited resources to meet *measurable* goals and objectives. Example: Teachers should be scheduled so that their talents are matched with student needs. So often in schools this is not the case. The new teacher usually gets the lower ability groups, the master teacher the higher academic students and little attention is given to scheduling students or teachers based on how well one is suited for the other.

By constantly evaluating the school schedule, the administration and staff can turn it into the school's most valuable resource. The procedure for evaluating is as follows:

- Do a needs assessment for the present schedule.
- Evaluate assessment concerns.
- Formulate objectives to meet needs assessment concerns.
- Implement new schedule.
- Design evaluation to measure objective progress.
- Establish final evaluation format.
- Make revisions based on evaluation data.

Once objectives for scheduling have been established, instruments can be developed to evaluate progress. The following evaluation form is designed to evaluate objectives derived from the needs assessment process.

Teacher Form #1

Schedule Resource Evaluation

Directions: Mark the column that best evaluates the progress made to date. Where you feel the question can not fully be answered by this method, add your comments at the bottom.

	Fully Accomplished	Mostly Accomplished	Partly Accomplished	Not Accomplished
To provide a one-half hour lunch period for teachers and students				
To eliminate unnecessary teacher supervision of study hall, cafeteria, restrooms, school grounds, etc.				
To increase the amount of instructional time offered students by shortening homeroom sessions				
To cut down on the number of different rooms any one teacher has to go to				
To provide double block sessions for Art, Industrial Art, Home Economics and Music				
To increase the number of co-curricular activity time slots by two each week				
To insure that no student has more than one study hall each day				
To free up teachers so that they may be available for students who need extra help				
To provide a common meeting time for departments				
To standardize a number of existing complex class rotations				

Comments:

Figure 13-1

Equally important to the total resource allocation operation is how effectively you utilize staff.

DETERMINING PRIORITY IN STAFF ASSIGNMENTS

The teaching staff of any school is its most valuable resource and should be utilized to its maximm potential. Staff assignment goals and objectives should be developed to reflect the most effective use of personnel based upon the known conditions and needs of the school. Once established, the goals and objectives should serve as criteria for evaluation purposes. The staff evaluation form below was prepared from a list of objectives for a staff assignment guideline worked out by a committee of teachers and administrators.

Administrator's
Form

Evaluating Staff Assignments

Directions: Place a X mark in the appropriate column. The following evaluation questions reflect criteria contained in our staff assignment guidebook.

	Usually	Always	Seldom	Never
1. Staff input is a resource used in determining assignments.				
2. A well-planned formula insures that staff-student ratio assignments are equalized.				
3. All staff share equally in assignments with regard to high, average and low-ability students.				

4. When considering assignments, teachers' talents are matched with student needs. ___

5. Care is taken to insure that non-academic assignments are equalized. ___

6. Teachers unable to handle certain assignments are offered inservice opportunities so that they may gain the skills required to perform these assignments in the future. ___

7. Total school assignment needs are considered when hiring new staff. ___

8. Allotments for staff preparation time are equalized. ___

9. Provisions for evaluating staff assignments are well defined. ___

Figure 13-2

Staff assignments and the school schedule have the most pronounced effect on the quality of teaching within a building. Next in line comes the use of space and facilities.

REORDING SPACE AND FACILITY PRIORITIES

By developing sound procedures designed to evaluate existing space and facility use, the administration can set the stage for a viable reallocation program. The following questions need to be answered:

1. What areas in the building are underused, if any?

2. What areas are overused, if any?

3. Are any classrooms undersubscribed because too few students are assigned to them?

4. If there are undersubscribed rooms, is there a valid reason for them?

5. Is there a master school plan to distribute students based upon known space and facility availability?

6. Has there been a space and facilities study done in the last five years?

7. Have goals and objectives been developed for space and facility use?

8. How well is the scheduling program coordinated with space and facility assignments?

9. Has any administrator been given responsibility for space and facility use?

10. What methods, if any, are utilized to evaluate space and facility use?

The answers to these questions will provide you or your school evaluation team with some valuable insights into existing conditions, and they should enable you to establish a program based on goals and objectives that can be readily evaluated.

Space and facility plans need to be evaluated each year before scheduling begins and a constant review of space should take place annually. The following space-facility identification and evaluation of needs chart is one approach that may be used in this area.

SPACE—FACILITY IDENTIFICATION AND EVALUATION OF NEEDS

Academic or other Subject Areas	Class Size Range	Room Sizes Needed Square Feet	Number of Rooms Needed	Number of Rooms Available	Equipment Okay Yes or No
Social Studies	25—30	750—900	6	*5	Yes
Science	22—28	900	6	6	**No
Math	26—30	750—900	6	6	Yes
English	25—30	750—900	6	*5	Yes
Industrial Arts	15—18	1400	2	1+	***No
Home Economics	15—18	1400	2	2	Yes

*Ongoing space problem requires teachers to use other subject area rooms when not in use.

**Short of laboratory stations in two science rooms.

Have to make do at this time.
***Still trying to purchase mobile equipment to complete the required six phase program.

Figure 13-3

Similar space-facility identification and evaluation of needs charts can readily be developed for grade level organization, departmental needs, storage space allocation and a number of other areas.

REALLOCATING MONIES

Money allocation, in the final analysis, provides less flexibility than all other allocation possibilities. We have already mentioned that salaries, fringe benefits, transportation, utilities, maintenance and other fixed costs consume approximately ninety-five to ninety-seven percent of your school buget. It is important, however, to evaluate the distribution of available money to ascertain with some semblance of reliability whether the dollar is producing equal to our conceptual expectations. To determine whether your school needs to consider a better money reallocation system, try answering the following questions.

Directions: Answer yes or no. More than two no's indicate a need to reexamine your approach to budget allocation.

	Yes	No
1. Budget allocations are presently based on long-range priorities (up to four years).		
2. Increases to grade levels or departments are on the basis of validated facts, not assumptions.		
3. There is a standard accepted method of deriving these facts.		
4. There is a school plan for equalizing cost ratios between programs and the number of students served by each program.		

5. Goals and objectives have been established for determining reallocation procedures. _____
6. Provisions for staff input in the decision-making process are established and utilized. _____
7. School administrators continue to acquire up-to-date expertise in the area of budget allocation. _____
8. When funds are reallocated to new or different programs, an evaluation of their use is part of the process. _____
9. Someone has been designated "decision-maker" to determine the effectiveness of money reallocation and utilization.

Figure 13-4

You should not be disillusioned into believing that budgetary allocations via this method will save schools substantial sums of money. Constant examination and evaluation of the budgetary process and school needs will allow for a more judicious distribution of money.

One method of evaluating the need for reallocating money and other resources is to compare actual student achievement with expected achievement as described in Chapter 8.

Resource Evaluation #6

Hopeville School

Grade Achievement Versus Expected Achievement

Explanation: Initial testing and other data indicates that all grades should be performing at an average level or better. Based on data compiled through mid-year, grade two may need additional resource help. Implications for next year's grade two budget are evident.

Grades performing above potential	3 4 6 7
Grades performing at potential	K 1 5 8
Grades performing below potential	2

Figure 13-5

REDISTRIBUTING TIME ALLOTMENTS

Another area that has a pronounced effect on how well a school operates is *time*. Are present allotments of time for staff, administration, and students adequate to reach stated school goals and objectives? What criteria determines how time is allotted? What measures are in effect to evaluate time allottments? These questions only reflect the surface of the many that could and should be asked. To begin the first stage of the time evaluation process, you, as principal, should examine the effectiveness of your own operation and that of other school administrators.

Evaluating Administrative Time Allottments: Most principals and other administrators get caught up in superfluous types of activities that prevent them from accomplishing more important tasks. The story of the principal who had to pardon himself five times to a visitor so he could listen to parents on the phone telling him why their children would not be in school that day was related to me as an example of unwise use of time. What things are you unable to do in school? Could you do them if you weren't doing several unimportant tasks? One way to answer these questions is to design your own evaluation task chart.

EVALUATION TASK CHART

Things I do	Should do	Shouldn't do	Things I don't do	Should do
1. Student absence excuses		X	1. Spend time talking to students	X
2. Discipline	X?		2. Order supplies	
3. Cafeteria duty		X	3. Staff duty rosters	
4. Department meetings	X		4. Evaluate special areas	X
5. School newsletter		X	5. Fill in	
6. Total schedule	X	X	6. " "	
7. Fill in			7. " "	
8. " "			8. " "	
9. " "			9. " "	
10. " "			10. " "	

Tasks I should add

_____

_____

_____

Tasks I should discard

_____

_____

_____

Figure 13-6

Other evaluative approaches should be utilized by you to evaluate the use of your own time. Several other evaluations displays can be found in a number of the books listed in the bibliography.

Evaluating Learning Time Allotments: Instructional time allotments are often the result of following some outmoded guideline or a decision left arbitrarily to the classroom teacher. Time allocations should be carefully planned, based on some evidence gathered which shows that it takes x number of hours per day, week and month to teach reading, math, biology or any other subject. Based upon a series of evaluation sessions, the White River Elementary School in Hartford, Vermont, developed a time allotment framework to be used as a guideline for meeting instructional objectives.

White River Elementary School

TIME ALLOTMENTS   3rd Grade

DAILY TIME ALLOTMENTS

	Teaching time	Other time	Total
8:30 - 10:30 Teaching time	120 min.		
10:30 - 10:45 Recess		15 min.	
10:45 - 12:00 Teaching time	75 min.		
12:00 - 12:40 Lunch & Recess		40 min.	
12:40 - 2:15 Teaching time	95 min.		
290 min.	290 min.	55 min.	
	or	or	
Daily teaching time	4 hr. 50 min.	55 min. =	5 hr. 45 min.
Weekly teaching time	× 5	× 5	× 5
	24 hr. 10 min.	4 hr. 35 min. =	28 hr. 45 min.

Minus

P.E.	40 min.	
Music	40 min.	
Art	40 min.	
Library	40 min.	2 hr. 40 min.
Total		21 hr. 30 min.

WEEKLY CLASSROOM TEACHING TIME

Reading Instruction	6 hr. 30 min.
Arith. Instruction	5 hr.
Language Arts	
Handwriting	1 hr.
Spelling	2 hr.
Creative Writing	2 hr.
Social Stud. & Science	
Instruction	5 hr.
TOTAL	21 hr. 30 min.

Figure 13-7

An elementary school example has been displayed, but the same need to evaluate time allotments for instructional purposes exists at the secondary level. Is there enough time allocated for writing skills? How do you know?

Evaluating Staff Time Allotments: Well-planned staff time allotments contribute considerably to school effectiveness. Time is one resource you, as principal, have some control over, and you should evaluate how well staff time allotments are being utilized in your school. The staff time allotment survey sheet enables the administration to do an initial evaluation overview of existing conditions.

IMPROVING THE ENVIRONMENTAL SETTING

How well children learn often depends on how they perceive their classroom setting. If their perception of the classroom is one of a bright, cheery place where a variety of materials and equipment are readily available, then learning has a good chance of taking place. If, on the other hand, students do not picture their classroom in this manner and also experience difficulty in iden-

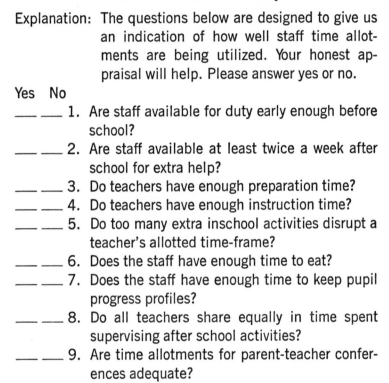

Administrator and
Department Head Form

Staff Time Allotment Survey

Explanation: The questions below are designed to give us an indication of how well staff time allotments are being utilized. Your honest appraisal will help. Please answer yes or no.

Yes No

____ ____ 1. Are staff available for duty early enough before school?

____ ____ 2. Are staff available at least twice a week after school for extra help?

____ ____ 3. Do teachers have enough preparation time?

____ ____ 4. Do teachers have enough instruction time?

____ ____ 5. Do too many extra inschool activities disrupt a teacher's allotted time-frame?

____ ____ 6. Does the staff have enough time to eat?

____ ____ 7. Does the staff have enough time to keep pupil progress profiles?

____ ____ 8. Do all teachers share equally in time spent supervising after school activities?

____ ____ 9. Are time allotments for parent-teacher conferences adequate?

Figure 13-8

tifying with the teacher or fellow classmates, learning may very well suffer. What constitutes a positive classroom and/or school environmental setting? How do you determine if you have a positive environmental setting?

Several fairly technical studies have been carried out by evaluators in this area and they may be referred to when seeking answers to the questions above. However, the uniqueness of each school somewhat dictates that these questions be answered through the combined efforts of faculty and administration. Determining the essential ingredients of a positive environmental setting should be the first order of business. Once this has been accomplished, the faculty and administration may then develop a program to evaluate existing environmental setting conditions. Further provisions for an ongoing evaluation program will help to insure that continual improvements will be made to the environmental setting.

EVALUATING THE TOTAL RESOURCE ALLOCATION CONCEPT

We have identified school resources as including: personnel, facilities, materials, equipment, time allotments, schedules, environment and money. Collectively, they comprise the resources available to a principal or designated administrator that may be allocated or reallocated in an effort to create a more effective school. To insure that maximum benefits are derived from the allocation of resources, each resource use must be evaluated and the evaluation data analyzed. Before individual resources can be upgraded, the needs must be ranked in order of priority. This is an evaluation process which looks at the total resource picture in an effort to determine which resources are in the most need of improvement by the greatest number of subject areas in school. Each department or grade level is measured. A sample science department allocation need chart follows.

RESOURCE ALLOCATION NEED CHART

Resources	SCIENCE DEPARTMENT									
	Least									Most
**Need	1	2	3	4	5	6	7	8	9	10
Personnel										
Facilities										
Materials										
Equipment										
Time Allot.										
Schedule										
Environment										
Dollars										

Figure 13-9

By inserting *All Departments* in the area marked *Science Department,* this form may be used as a total department tally sheet to ascertain the apparent greatest resource needs of the school. Example:

RESOURCE ALLOCATION NEED CHART

	Resources	All Departments
	Least		Most

**Need	1	2	3	4	5	6	7	8	9	10

Personnel
Facilities
Materials

Figure 13-10

SUMMARY

An awareness that school resources will have to be reallocated to meet future needs is essential. The master schedule and staff assignments represent your true ability to manuver limited resources to meet measurable goals and objectives. Space and facilities are another major area that can be evaluated and put to maximum use.

Constant examination and evaluation of the budgetary process and school needs will allow for a more judicious distribution of money. Time allotments should be evaluated for administrative duties, learning opportunities and staff operations. To insure that maximum benefits are derived from the allocation of resources, each resource use must be evaluated and decisions made based on evaluation results.

BIBLIOGRAPHY

Articles:

Forster, Fred, "How To Push Through Better Evaluation Programs," *Nation's Schools*, 88 July 1971, pp. 27-28.

Gmelch, Walter H. "Evaluation: Diagnosis or Decree," *Catalyst For Change,* Journal of the National School Development Council, Vol. 6 No. 2, Winter 1977.

Hogben, Donald. "Curriculum Development and Evaluation: The Need to Look Beyond Behavioral Objectives," *Teacher's College Record*, 74 May 1973, pp. 529-536.

Howsam, Robert B. "Current Issues in Evaluation," *National Elementary Principal*, February 1973, pp. 12-17.

Karns, Edward A. and Wenger, Marilyn J. "Developing Corrective Evaluation Within The Program," *Educational Leadership*, March 1973, pp. 533-535.

Meyers, Donald A. "Improved Decision Making For School Organization. What and What For," *National Elementary Principal*, January 1973, pp. 43-50.

Stufflebeam, Daniel L. "The Relevance of the CIPP Evaluation Model for Educational Accountability" *Journal of Research and Development in Education* V February 1971, pp. 19-25.

Books:

Dunn, Rita and Kenneth J. "Administrators Guide to New Programs for Faculty Management and Evaluation," West Nyack, N.Y., Parker Publishing Co., Inc., 1977.

English, Fenwick W. and Kaufman, Roger A. "Needs Assessment, A Guide to Improve School District Management," Arlington, Virginia, American Association of School Administrators, 1976.

Frank, John H. "Complete Guide to Co-curricular Programs and Activities for the Middle Grades," West Nyack, N. Y., Parker Publishing Co., Inc., 1976 (Chapter 10).

Herman, Jerry J. "Developing an Effective Staff Evaluation Program," West Nyack, N. Y., Parker Publishing Co., Inc., 1973.

Houts, Paul L. "The Myth of Measurability," New York, Hart Publishing Co., Inc., 1977.

Hyman, Ronald T. "School Administrators Handbook of Teacher Supervision and Evaluation Methods," Englewood Cliffs, N. J., Prentice-Hall, Inc., 1975.

Olds, Robert H. "Administrative and Supervisory Evaluation," Arlington, Virginia, American Association of School Administrators, 1977.

Popham, James W. (Editor) "Evaluation in Education," Berkley, California, McCutchan Publishing Corporation, 1974.

Popham, James W. "Educational Evaluation," Englewood Cliffs, N. J., Prentice-Hall, Inc., 1975.

Walberg, Herbert J. (Editor) "Evaluating Educational Performance," Berkley, California, McCutchan Publishing Corporation, 1974.

INDEX